Things You Wish You Knew Yesterday

and other stuff you'll need to know tomorrow

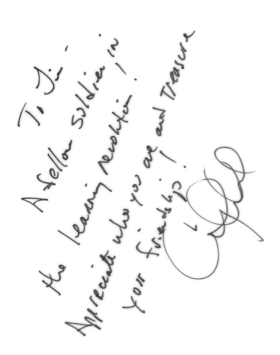

To Ji -

A fellow soldier in
the learning revolution!
Appreciate who you are and treasure
your friendship!

Book Cover Text: Graham Van Dixhorn, Write to Your
Market, Inc.

ISBN: 978-0-9908214-0-3

Printed in USA by Midland Institute Press

Praise for
Things You Wish You Knew Yesterday

"Craig's ideas, perspective and vision for developing future leaders and entrepreneurs is life-changing. I hope that you take the time to read this book and then buy one for every young person you know because it will be time and money well spent."

> Sarah Petty, owner Joy of Marketing and New York Times Best Selling author of *Worth Every Penny*

"I can never "un-learn" these life lessons; they will forever influence the way I view and interact with the world around me."

> Amelia Winters, (former student)

"This book has all the things I wish I had known growing up. Where was Mr. Lindvahl's class when I needed it!?!"

> Michael Buchanan~Writer for the feature documentary Spiral Bound
> Co-author/screenwriter of The Fat Boy Chronicles
> *Winner of 2010 Mom's Choice Gold Award, National Parenting Publications Gold Award for Teens and NY Champions of Character Award*

"Craig Lindvahl's life lessons as a classroom teacher are a thing of legend. Thanks to this book, his classroom just got a little bigger."

> Joe Fatheree, Illinois Teacher of the Year 2007

"Craig hits the nail on the head. Time after time, drawing from real life experiences on the front lines, in the trenches, and atop mountains, Craig has composed a packed manual for how to get the most out of life and hack your way to success. Hint: it's not what you think!"

> Ted Gonder, CEO of Moneythink and youngest appointed advisor to the U.S. President

"Craig Lindvahl understands the millennial generation and what makes them tick better than anyone I have ever come in contact with. Simply put, this book lays the groundwork to guide Generation Y in successfully handling the crazy thing we call life. Craig's passion for teaching his life lessons to youth has also spilled over to the many adults and businesses who have heard his message. This is a must read for all ages."

Jack Schultz
Author, *Boomtown USA*
Ernst and Young Entrepreneur of the Year

TABLE OF CONTENTS

Seeing The Big Picture

Changing The Way You Think

Thinking About How You Say It

Table of Contents

Understanding Other People

Learning From Other People

Things You Wish You Knew Yesterday

DEDICATION

This book is dedicated to everyone connected with the CEO (Creating Entrepreneurial Opportunities) program. Whether you were part of the original group in Effingham, Illinois, or you're a facilitator, student, alumni, investor, board member, or school administrator, you are transforming lives and communities through your work.

Thank you.

Things You Wish You Knew Yesterday

FOREWORD

Meggie Zahneis

This is not one of *those* books.

Trust me.

Believe me—I've endured tons of preachy, teachy sermons from well-intentioned adults who promise their missives will *change your life!*

Except then they don't.

Craig Lindvahl isn't like that.

I first met Craig in the spring of 2012, on Opening Day for baseball's Cincinnati Reds. Around Cincinnati, Opening Day is a big deal—practically a local holiday—and I was lucky enough to experience my first Opening Day as a member of the working media that year, after being hired as Major League Baseball's Youth Correspondent in the fall of 2011. I was fourteen years old and desperate to capture every moment as I stood on the field during pregame festivities. All was going according to plan ... until the AA batteries in my rinky-dink point-and-shoot camera died (a predictable outcome, given my tendency to keep my finger on the shutter button at all times).

So there I was, rummaging frantically through my bag

in search of spares when Craig walked up. I'd never seen him before, but when he offered me a few extra batteries from his stash, a friendship blossomed.

In the past few years, Craig has become a second father to me. We've found that we have a lot in common—a love of baseball and of creativity, a passion for filmography and photography, plenty of experience being the weirdest person in the room, and a wonderfully biting and self-deprecating, sarcastic sense of humor—and my admiration for Craig as a professional and as a person has only grown the more I learn about the incredible life he's led.

With thirty-four years of teaching—everything from kindergarten to twelfth grade and every subject from band and music to filmmaking and entrepreneurship—dozens of documentaries (written, filmed, and produced), and twelve Mid-America Emmys under his belt, not to mention a successful public speaking career and a position as executive director of a thriving entrepreneurship institute, Craig has a lot of life experience to draw on.

And I feel lucky that he's chosen to impart some of that valuable life knowledge to me. Craig has shared the life lessons in this book with me at one point or another, whether during a long phone call as he's traveled across the country on speaking engagements or via email when I've just been having a rough day.

So I can endorse Craig and this book wholeheartedly. If Craig says something has the power to change your life, it will change your life. Because Craig is that kind of guy. He just *gets* it: the way we think, feel, and act, what makes us tick, our triumphs and our tribulations … Craig Lindvahl is a man with his finger on the pulse of humanity.

The thing is, Craig's going to tell it like it is. Because he doesn't believe in all the flowery crap and BS drivel lots of self-help books will try to hit you over the head with. That's a rare gift. Not only that, but he just plain makes sense. His advice is both prescient and practical, and while he'll tell you he's no inspiration, you'll beg to differ once you get to know him a bit.

That's why you need this book.

Just open it up and give it a try.

And you'll see that *Things You Wish You Knew Yesterday* isn't one of *those* books.

Trust me.

Meggie Zahneis
Youth Correspondent
Major League Baseball
MLB.com

INTRODUCTION

I've spent the last thirty-five years working as a teacher, filmmaker, and musician. I've had an odd life, to be sure.

I've filmed in places as diverse as Times Square, the Tetons, and Abraham Lincoln's home, and interviewed people as diverse as politicians, authors, Medal of Honor recipients, and Major League Baseball players. I've met celebrities, CEOs, and people from all over the world.

I've also filmed on little league ball diamonds, in people's barns, and in the woods by my house, and I've interviewed farmers, plumbers, and five-year-old kids. I've met church choir members, night janitors, and kids, also from all over the world.

I've taught kids in every grade from K–12, several thousand of them. They graciously allowed me to share a portion of their lives and gave me more than I could ever offer them.

My life has been rich and blessed by the opportunity to observe and learn from every situation and every person I've ever encountered. Most of what I know about what is right and good has come from those observations, and from them I developed a series of what my students came to know as "The Life Lessons". I shared these, in one form or another, with the students I taught, no matter the grade or subject. I did so because a good life lesson will shed light on a hundred different parts of your life. A good life lesson is essential truth, and it can apply to almost anything.

A good life lesson causes people to:

- Have a revelation
- See it all around them
- Change their behavior

You experience a good life lesson, and you think, "Hmmm, I never thought about it like that." Over the next few days, you're amazed at how often you see it, and you ask yourself, "How could I have been blind to this?" Once you know what you know, you can't go back to not knowing. See?

Once you know how to be a success in life, you can do darn near anything. People will be drawn to you, you'll have the confidence and poise to follow your dreams and ideas, and you'll see opportunities where others see only risk.

You'll find a lot of crossover between the life lessons in this book. Somehow school teaches us that we do things just once, and if things come around again we say, "Hey, we already did this!" Sometimes thinking about the same point two or three different ways gives you a perspective that drives home the point. Sometimes you read something again six months later and it takes on a whole new meaning. Sometimes you read something and you're just not ready to learn it. You happen on the same point again and think, "How could I have missed this?!?"

What you'll find here are simple lessons that can move you far beyond your peers. Whether you're sixteen or sixty, these are universal truths that will change the way you think, act, and interact.

Although I taught music, band, filmmaking, and entrepreneurship, these life lessons were always at the center of every class. When kids tell me, years later, they still remember what I taught them, it's almost never about music, filmmaking, or entrepreneurship; what they remember is what they learned about *life*.

I hope you'll feel the same way.

Introduction

Things You Wish You Knew Yesterday

SEEING THE BIG PICTURE

Thinking big has a way of bringing the small stuff into focus.

Things You Wish You Knew Yesterday

PEOPLE

This is the first chapter in the book for a reason. If you don't buy into this idea, you're not going to get much from the rest of the book. Every single one of the most successful people I know practices this idea, and nearly every one of the least successful people I've met steadfastly refuses to consider it.

Entrepreneurial thinkers look at the world and see exciting things to do, experience, learn, and accomplish everywhere! So do most little kids. I've taught kids in every grade from K–12, and one of the things I love most about teaching kids in kindergarten is that they're excited about *everything*. The world is just the most interesting thing they can imagine, and they can't wait to explore it.

If you ask a group of kindergartners, "Who knows about nuclear physics?" Every hand goes in the air.

And not just in the air, but thrust up in the air so hard that you think their arms will pop out of their shoulder joints.

The hands are also accompanied by the "ooh … ooh … ooh" sound that means every kid is desperate to tell you something. If you call on one, saying, "Okay, John-  ny, what do you know about nuclear physics?" the response goes something like, "Ummm … uhhh … I … this one time … and you know what else … I … ummm … uhhh … and … I saw a puppy."

In the end, it's easy to understand that kindergartners just want to tell you *something*. It doesn't matter if it's related to whatever you're doing. They're just excited about life, curious about everything, and they want to be engaged.

If you ask a group of first graders, "Who can help me solve a problem?" nearly every hand goes up. Not just raised hands, but hands raised in a way that says, "Heck yeah, I can solve problems. That's what I *do*."

And when a six-year-old asks questions about things, they're usually pretty darn good questions. Deep questions.

By the middle of second grade, though, most of them have learned there's no need to be curious. We're

going to tell them exactly what they need to now. They've pretty much stopped asking questions, because they've learned that asking questions is a negative, not a positive.

I find it fascinating that students will make fun of the kid who's brave enough to ask the question, because on the inside they're thinking, "Boy, am I glad you asked that. I have no idea what we're supposed to do. I'm just glad you're the one getting made fun of, not me."

By high school, students have learned that the game of school goes like this: Students get fed the same stuff at the same time.

They burp some of it back up on a test, and if it looks kind of like what went in, they move on.

The stuff that wasn't on the test gets urped back up into the netherworld where all extra knowledge goes,

I guess, and then the class moves on.

Knowledge and information, then, are things that have an immediate and specific purpose. You gather and store things in your mind for a test or quiz, and then you forget them. The test or quiz is the reason for learning those things, after all, so why would you carry them in your mind?

Over the course of years they spend in school, students easily find their view of the world becoming more and more narrow. By the time they're in high school and college, the same world that excited them in kindergarten looks very different.

The curtain closes a little at a time until most of the exciting parts of learning and life are no longer visible. If information doesn't connect with an immediate need, it becomes irrelevant and non-existent. You hear students say things like, "I don't see why I have to know this. This is stupid. I'll never need it."

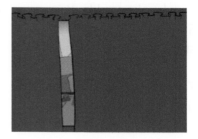

When you develop such a narrow view of the world, it's logical that you can't connect what you're learning with what you might need to know, isn't it?

It's completely understandable. There are lots of people who see the world this way, and I feel sorry for them. When your curtains close and your view narrows, it's easy to be negative, easy to be cynical. I promise you the rest of that wonderful world is still out there. You just have to open the curtains again.

The most successful people I know retain that wide-eyed view of the world. They continue to see it as a place of opportunity and promise. That's where great, new ideas come from.

Gregg Lohman is one of those people. When he first entered my classroom, he was a shy, ten-year-old fifth grader. When I say shy, I mean he basically didn't speak to me. He wanted to be a drummer, though, and I knew there was something special about this kid from the first lesson.

He did absolutely everything I suggested to him. Everything. If I had suggested he rub gravel in his hair because it would make him a better drummer, he would have done it. He was willing to do anything to be a better musician and was quite content to take in anything I offered, accept it, and sort it out later. I think he knew some things would be more valuable than others, but he didn't want to take the chance on missing something that might help him improve.

At the start of his senior year in high school, he decided he wanted to do what was necessary to be named an "All-State" musician. It's an incredibly difficult thing to accomplish; it requires a musician to compete with students from all around the state.

To become an All-State percussionist, one must show proficiency on a number of instruments. Snare drum, timpani, marimba, and multi-percussion are all part of the audition process. Gregg was already great on the snare drum, but really hadn't explored the other instruments.

Mastering these instruments normally takes years and years. Gregg mastered them all in a couple of months. The approach to learning that had served him so well as a fifth grader prepared him to absorb a remarkable amount of information in a very short time.

His work ethic allowed him to get more out of each minute of practice than others gained from a week. In two short months, he auditioned and was selected to move to the state round. There, Gregg would compete with students from all over Illinois, many of them students who had studied with some of the finest instructors in the country. Nearly all of them had years more experience than Gregg.

Well, that young man finished his audition and came away ranked as the #2 percussionist in the state of Illinois. And you know what? It didn't surprise me one bit.

After high school, he decided to become a drummer in Nashville, to make his way in the world of country music. During college, he regularly drove seventy-five miles to a small country music theater. But he didn't go to see the show.

He parked in the parking lot and waited for the drummer to go from the tour bus to the theater. He built his network of contacts one at a time, introducing himself to musicians and taking in whatever advice they might offer.

It's probably obvious that a number of universities were anxious to have Gregg attend their institutions to get a master's degree. He chose the University of Tennessee because of its proximity to Nashville and the presence of a particular professor.

As you've no doubt guessed, he drove to Nashville on weekends to listen in the clubs and meet more people. That's actually how he got his first opportunity in Nashville. His roommate, a bass player, invited him to sit in one evening. In Nashville, it's not unusual for the house band in a club to invite aspiring musicians to hop up on stage and sit in for a tune. It's sort of a baptism by fire.

I cannot imagine, not for the life of me, what it must have been like the first time this shy, quiet, young man jumped up on a stage to sit in.

It didn't go particularly well. He wasn't familiar with all the terminology Nashville musicians use, and they were playing an old song he didn't know. He was confused, he was nervous, he didn't know the tune—but he played.

Then he went out and bought a bunch of old country albums and listened and learned, and the next time it went much better. He started sitting in more often and was eventually offered a house job, where he played 5–6 hours a few nights a week. He worked all day for a musician, then taught drum lessons, then went and played in the clubs until 2:00 in the morning, then started all over again the next day.

He began to build a reputation as a great drummer, but more importantly, he built a reputation as a great human being. He was a great listener, a superb learner, and a guy who did the right things and did them well.

Gregg soon found himself working regularly around Nashville and has been the drummer and bandleader for Kellie Pickler since 2006. He's toured all over the world and experienced a life that you and I could only dream of.

It wasn't quite as simple as all that. I'm leaving out most of the hard parts, of course. The most difficult chapter came in March 2013. I received a call on my cell phone from Gregg's number. It was a state trooper calling to try and identify the owner of Gregg's phone. Gregg had been in a horrible car accident in Louisville, KY, and his phone was found at the accident scene.

I asked the trooper, "Is he okay?"

The trooper responded, "It's bad."

I asked, "Is he going to live?"

All the trooper could say was, "It's bad … it's really, really bad."

Gregg was actually passed over for dead. It was only after the emergency responders heard him gasp that they knew he was still alive. The myriad of injuries he suffered, including a broken neck, should have been fatal. I'll never forget what I saw the next morning when I walked into the intensive care unit of the hospital in Louisville. Since that day in 1987 when we first met, Gregg has become a part of our family. My wife and I consider him our adopted son, and we're forever grateful to his family for sharing him with us. Seeing him on a ventilator, with all the tubes and wires connected to him, is a sight I'll never quite get over.

Later in this book you'll find a lesson about personal capital. It's the capital you build by living your life the right way, doing the right things and doing them well.

Gregg received huge dividends from his personal capital account, and out of this horrific situation came something wonderful. Gregg had the opportunity to experience the overwhelming love and concern from family, friends, and the music community in Nashville. He had no idea he'd had that kind of impact on so many.

I'll also never forget the night, a couple of months after the accident, when Gregg surprised Kellie Pickler by playing drums for the first time. He waited until the encore, and when Kellie returned to the stage, Gregg was there, playing. It was difficult for her to get through the song, and the hug she gave Gregg after that was as emotional as anything I've ever witnessed.

Gregg is now determined to take what he's learned from this horrible experience and use it to make others better. And you know what? That's exactly what he'll do.

When you take it all in, when you seek to learn from everyone and everything, you're not limited by circumstances, geography, age, or anything else. You'll wonder why everyone can't see the same possibilities for themselves. You'll do things in your life that others can't even imagine, and you'll wonder why it's such a big deal.

As you read the rest of this book, do me a favor, okay? Take it all in. Look beyond the moment, look beyond your present circumstances. Look at your life as the incredible gift it is, and look at yourself as the unique gift you are to the world.

You know how a magnifying glass distorts things? Things in the middle, where the magnifying power is focused, appear much larger than their actual size. Your brain houses a magnifying lens of sorts. Information, knowledge, life events, other people, how you feel about things, stress—all those things slide under that magnifying glass and are given a level of importance in your life.

Never forget that the things you focus the lens on appear to be the biggest and most important things in your life. Because you choose where to aim the lens, it's a pretty subjective thing.

The things that happen in our lives, like challenges, obstacles, and successes, are mostly objective. The way we perceive them is subjective. Our perception is what we use to magnify them. Make sense?

Let's say you take an important test, and you get a crummy grade.

A completely objective observer would say, "They took a test and received a D." Period.

The corresponding thoughts

of "My life is over," "I'll never get to college," "I'm a complete failure," and "I always do this when it matters most," are all thoughts *you* add to the mix.

When you're "thinking right," everything seems proportional. You're not overwhelmed by situations you face and, while you may not like every person you deal with, your relationships are workable. You're not resentful over problems that arise, and you feel like you have the resources you need to deal with them.

When you're "thinking right," your magnifying glass is aimed at the good and positive parts of your life. The negative things seem much smaller.

When you're not "thinking right," things are out of whack. You're resentful of the problems you face, and the people you meet seem to get in the way—life is just more complicated. Your magnifying glass slips, it focuses on negative and unhappy parts of your life, and they become *huge*.

In my life, for instance, I want to be a great filmmaker. It's obvious that technology, budgeting, storyboarding, hiring the right crew, working on the script, and editing are all necessary components, right? Those things are all out there on the edge somewhere, hardly noticeable. That's because my magnifying glass is trained on the important things, like the story, the people in the film, the purpose of the film, and the satisfaction of working on the project.

When I start thinking about how busy I am and start asking myself things like, "How long will this take?" or

"How much work will this be?" then I know I'm in trouble. When something minor comes along and I think, "This is all I freakin' need!" then I know the problem is me. That's when I know things are out of whack and I'm losing sight of what's really important.

Isn't it amazing how quickly we can go from feeling like we're on top of things, completely in control, to feeling like we're completely under water? Just know that the list of things we want to stay on top of doesn't really change. We re-aim the magnifying glass, and our perception changes. When it does, the list looks entirely different.

Meggie Zahneis is probably the best "magnifier" I've ever met. She has had an incredible life, and she has every right to look at things in a pretty unpleasant way.

Meggie was born with HSANII, which is a neurological disorder that means she doesn't feel pain and temperature the same way other people do. She's one of about fifty people in the world who have HSANII.

Did I mention she's deaf? She has cochlear implants in both ears, but you'd never really know she has a hearing problem. I have no idea how she does it.

Did I mention she's had more than a dozen major surgeries to correct various situations?

Did I mention that she has restless leg syndrome so severely that she almost never gets any REM sleep?

Need I go further?

It bugs me when I hear professional athletes talk about adversity. Too often, they're talking about self-inflicted circumstances like drugs, scrapes with the law, and other consequences of their own stupidity. At seventeen, Meggie's been through more real adversity than most of us will experience in a lifetime. This is a young person who has every right to look at life through the lens of her disabilities. I wouldn't blame her a bit for focusing her magnifying glass squarely on her difficulties.

She doesn't, though. She just doesn't. As you might guess, she spent a lot of time in the hospital during her childhood. She became a voracious reader and writer, and because of that her intellect is far beyond that of most people her age.

When she was in the eighth grade, Meggie entered a writing contest sponsored by Major League Baseball and the Jackie Robinson family. Hers was one of 1,500 entries from all across the United States. When Sharon Robinson (Jackie's daughter) called to let her know she'd won, Meggie's jaw dropped, and a new career was launched.

Bud Selig, the commissioner of baseball, liked her work so much he hired her to be the youth correspondent for Major League Baseball's web presence, MLB.com. At fourteen, Meggie found herself catapulted from being an eighth grader to working in the role of a major league sportswriter. She's worked the World Series, All-Star games, and has interviewed many of the biggest names in baseball.

I spent several seasons doing behind-the-scenes documentaries with the Cincinnati Reds, and that's how I met Meggie. We met at the ballpark in Cincinnati one Opening Day and have been fast friends ever since. In fact, we collaborated on a film together. It's called *A Ballpark Story: From the End to the Beginning*, a behind-the-scenes look at how the Cincinnati Reds create a terrific experience for fans at Great American Ballpark in Cincinnati. The film is available on MLB.com under the title *Diamond Stories: GABP*.

Meggie is the host, co-writer, and co-producer. Pretty amazing stuff for someone with two years of high school left to complete.

She's not perfect, by the way. Sometimes things get out of balance. Sometimes stuff just gets to her. She's operating at the highest levels of her profession, but she's still a high school student—that's not easy. Her body often works against her, and things that you and I take for granted are a major effort for her.

That's when she goes back to her magnifying lens and takes a look at what threw off her aim. The great thing about Meggie is that she never loses sight of who she wants to be. She knows that she wants, through her life and work, to inspire and motivate, to truly make a difference in people's lives. That clear vision makes it possible to get back on track, whether that requires a bit of a tweak or a major overhaul.

I love that about her. Being imperfect means she's normal. Sometimes we put people on a pedestal and pretend they're infallible. It's normal to have moments, or days, when you aren't the person you'd like to be. You shouldn't expect to get your magnifying glass aimed and expect it to stay that way forever. Meggie totally gets that and is willing to adjust as often as needed.

If you're clear on what matters and keep your magnifying glass aimed at that, you can weather the difficult times. You can tackle big, hairy goals in your life because you'll have the ability to keep things in perspective. You can adjust your aim as often as you need to, as significantly as you need to.

It's a simple thought, but you can't imagine how profound it is.

Or maybe you can.

Things You Wish You Knew Yesterday

LIFE AIN'T NO LASER BEAM

zzzzING!

When you're a senior in high school, life can be full of complicated decisions. It's easy to approach those decisions with a great deal of fear and anxiety. "What if I choose the wrong school? What if I choose the wrong major?" You're afraid you'll waste valuable time, waste the money you or your parents invest in your schooling, or set yourself on a course that won't produce success and happiness in your life.

I have no idea why, but many of the high school students I've worked with over the years have the crazy perception that life is going to happen in a straight line.

As you get older, the same fear exists when it comes to making decisions, but it tends to be in smaller doses. You may not feel like a particular decision will throw the rest of your life into disarray, but the fear of making the wrong decision can certainly paralyze you. You can find yourself stuck in a loop, going over and over and over the possible consequences of the decision until you can't move.

That's why the decisions about whether or not to go to college, which college to attend, and which major to choose become such huge issues. There's a feeling that you're making an irrevocable decision, that it's a straight line from that moment to the end of your working life.

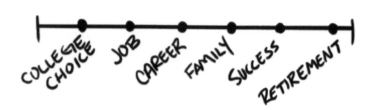

You want to know what life is *really* like?

If you ask a hundred forty-year-old professionals, you might be surprised at how many of them will tell you they're doing something completely different than they prepared for in college. It's certainly true in my life.

I never, *ever* thought I'd be doing what I'm doing. If you had asked me when I was twenty years old, I would have told you that I'd be working today in Los Angeles as a studio musician and composer.

You know what's interesting, though? I'm not doing that, but I'm NOT disappointed. I'm doing everything I always hoped I'd do, just not in any of the ways I thought I might.

In my creative life, I didn't end up working as a studio musician in Los Angeles, but I've done studio work elsewhere, and I've worked as a composer. I became a documentary filmmaker, and that allows me to write music for stories I like, and it's allowed me to add other creative skills, like cinematography, editing, and writing. I've done films on a huge variety of topics, from Vietnam to mountain climbing to Abraham Lincoln to baseball, and met some incredible people while working on those projects.

I've also spent several seasons doing behind-the-scenes documentaries with the Cincinnati Reds. I could never have guessed that I would end up working in Major League Baseball! In the end, I've done precisely what I always wanted to do creatively. It's just that I could never have predicted it would have worked out like this, and it *definitely* wasn't a straight line.

In my life as a teacher, I spent a long time teaching music, then filmmaking, and finally entrepreneurship. In the last several years of my teaching career, I wasn't teaching anything I went to college to prepare to teach. Definitely not a laser beam straight line—I mean how could I, armed with a music degree, have imagined that I would finish my career teaching filmmaking and entrepreneurship?

It's interesting, though, that there was a laser beam straight line through all of my teaching. No matter the subject or the age of the students, what I really taught all those years was *life*. I was always trying to teach students how to be successful in life. That was at the heart of everything I did. It's why I stayed in teaching.

In 2008, I was given the opportunity to take a completely different path in education with the launch of an entrepreneurship class that became known as CEO (Creating Entrepreneurial Opportunities). It's an entrepreneurship class, but it's really about becoming a successful person. If you manage to do that, the rest of life sort of takes care of itself.

So in the end, my life has been all over the place. Music and filmmaking have taken me all over the world and given me experiences, friendships, and opportunities far beyond my wildest imaginings. None of those things came in ways I could have predicted.

Niall and Kristie Campbell are perfect examples, and I never would've met them if I'd been working at some studio in L.A. They own a terrific restaurant called Firefly Grill in the small town of Effingham, Illinois. It's the kind of eatery you'd find in a trendy part of San Francisco, or maybe New York City. It's very odd to find it nestled amid the cornfields in a community of twelve thousand people. Their path to Firefly Grill wasn't a laser beam, nor was the path that brought them together.

Kristie didn't necessarily find school an interesting place, but she was driven to succeed. She ended up working in the world of Wall Street and was extremely successful, both professionally and financially. She wasn't thinking marriage or children, she was thinking career.

Niall—well, Niall had done a number of things. Never a particularly interested student, Niall had devoted his life to adventure. He'd worked on a fishing boat in Alaska, wandered the country, and landed in Puerto Rico, working as a chef. Niall is a born entrepreneur, and he knew he wanted to own a restaurant at some point. His dream was to use his own imagination and ideas to create culinary experiences for people.

There's no way life could connect these two people, right? Until the attacks on 9/11, they were living in completely separate universes. On the morning of 9/11, Niall was scheduled to fly from Boston's Logan Airport to Newark, then on to England for a new job. Because of last minute visa issues, Niall decided not to fly that day. The world changed that morning, and in the wake of 9/11, a new work visa for his job in England was delayed for months, so Niall returned to Puerto Rico.

Kristie, too, was changed by 9/11, but in a different manner. Losing a number of friends in the attack caused her to begin to rethink her life. She asked herself, "If someone blew me up right now, is this where I would want to be?" The answer was no, and she knew she needed time to reevaluate and refocus her life. She decided to take a leave from her position and moved to Puerto Rico. It wasn't an easy decision. She occupied an enviable position on Wall Street—so enviable there were two thousand applicants for her position when she resigned.

Out of that horrific experience, though, came something wonderful. Kristie and Niall met in Puerto Rico, fell in love, and decided to move back to the United States.

When she took a leave of absence, Kristie had stored most of her belongings in Effingham, Illinois, where she had family. The newly engaged couple came through Effingham to pick up her stuff, and Kristie's father introduced them to some local businesspeople. Turns out they had been talking about the need for a gourmet restaurant in Effingham. They felt the right kind of restaurant would provide an incentive for businesses to locate in Effingham, make it easier to recruit executive talent to the area and attract diners from a wide area.

Kristie says it all makes sense, looking back. "These people had been looking for someone to do this, and we happened along at just the right moment. We understood immediately that this is the place that gave us the best shot at success—there was a need and a network of people to help make it happen," she said.

So, even though neither of them grew up there, or intended to settle there, Kristie and Niall built their dream restaurant in Effingham. They'd never done anything like that, mind you, had no experience designing a building or running a restaurant, but they jumped into the new adventure.

They each bring their own perspective to the endeavor. Niall feels he owes a debt of gratitude to the restaurant business. He had a very difficult upbringing, full of abuse, drugs, and alcohol. The food business gave him direction, and he feels it saved his life at some very pivotal moments. Because of his incredibly varied life experience, he's able to teach his employees about much more than food. He's helping them acquire critical life skills that will change the trajectory of their lives.

Kristie's primary motivator is to nourish and care for people, using Firefly Grill as the apparatus. For instance, she and Niall have made it their mission to utilize locally produced ingredients as often as possible, and farms have started around the area specifically to supply the Firefly. She's active in the community, and they've both decided that Effingham is not a stop along the highway of their lives; it's the place they want to call home.

They've resisted opportunities to expand Firefly Grill to other locations, resisted the temptation to take their success and transplant it to a major city. Niall says, "I get to get up in the morning and do what I love doing. Nothing's better than that."

It's not always easy. Like every business, they've had some dark moments. "It's a roller coaster, and you might as well just enjoy the ride," says Kristie. "When we have dark moments, we just think about the fact that we're doing exactly what we want to do, and that gets us through."

Are these two fabulously successful people? You bet. Did they take a straight, laser beam line to find each other? Not even close. Did they follow a laser beam path to Firefly Grill? Nope.

It makes sense looking back, though, doesn't it? Precious little of life happens in a straight line, and that's a good thing. Entrepreneurial thinkers are constantly aware of new ideas, new opportunities, and new possibilities. All of that leads you where you're supposed to go, but definitely not in a straight line.

The truth is this—you can look backward from your current position in life, and the path to where you are makes perfect sense. It's usually such a weird path that you could never suggest to someone else that they try and follow it. That's why, when you ask someone how they achieved their position in life, they often seem reluctant to share it with you as a road map.

Each experience in your life moves you a step closer to where you're supposed to be.

The key is to be a successful *person*. That's the most critical and difficult thing. What a successful person does with their professional career is a detail, don't you see? Whatever they do will be done well, and it will matter. Successful people do successful things, and those things make a positive difference to the people around them.

It's simple, but it's a huge deal. If you can understand this perspective, you'll gain the freedom to grow, explore, discover, and set yourself on a path that will turn the rest of your life into an exciting adventure.

Things You Wish You Knew Yesterday

RIDING THE RAPIDS

Ever take a ride down a river that has rapids? Sometimes you see them coming, sometimes you don't.

Sometimes you can see the rough water coming. The river's moving too fast, though, and you couldn't get off if you wanted.

And you want.

To get off.

Really bad.

You just have to acknowledge that it's going to be scary for a little while. You're going to feel like things are moving too fast, and things are happening far beyond your ability to control.

Then you hit the rapids, and it's like the world is moving in slow motion. You're tossed this way and that, and you're afraid you're going to fall out. You're afraid if you fall out, you'll never get back in!

You're cursing the day you ever got in this stupid boat. You're cursing the day you even heard about this stupid river. You're not sure you'll get through this. You're not sure it's *possible* to get through this.

And then you do.

You might feel a little beat up, a little disheveled, but you made it. And then comes the whoop of exhilaration. You feel like you can do anything.

And then you notice, up ahead, around the next corner. More rapids.

Oh freakin' no.

Same thing as before, but you curse the boat a little less, curse the river a little less, and feel the exhilaration a little more. You realize that most of your anxiety comes from *anticipating* what might happen, not by *experiencing* what happens as you ride the rapids. As you gain more confidence that things will be okay in the end, you kind of, sort of, even enjoy the fear.

Life is like that. You're on the river and you can't get off. There are going to be rapids, some you can see waiting for you, and some you can't. You have no choice, really, so you may as well accept it and enjoy the ride. You do have a choice, though, whether you feel only the anxiety and fear that come with anticipating the rapids or the excitement and exhilaration that come from riding them.

A good friend of mine, Kyle Packer, has lived this in both real and symbolic ways. Kyle was born with cerebral palsy, and the rapids in his life have been longer and more frequent than you and I can imagine.

Cerebral palsy is an interesting disability. Everyone who has CP is affected differently by it, and in Kyle's case, his speech and fine motor skills are most affected. He has limited use of his hands and cannot walk, except on his knees.

The best way to explain it is this: when you want to reach out and grab something, your eyes work with your brain to extend an arm, grip the thing, and pull it back. It doesn't require conscious thought. There's a disconnect that occurs between Kyle's brain, his arm, his hand, and his fingers. The message doesn't get delivered, or at least delivered in the right way. Moving his arm requires tremendous concentration and effort on Kyle's part. Moving any part of his body requires that same kind of concentration.

Kyle has chosen to ride the rapids, though, and sometimes seems to choose the branches of the river of life that have nothing but rapids! I've never met anyone more willing to embrace challenges.

When he was a college student, Kyle went on an eighteen-day, 257-mile rafting trip down the Colorado River. On the seventh day, the group knew they'd be running Crystal Rapid, the biggest rapid on the river.

There was reason to be anxious about the day. Crystal is dangerous, the most dangerous part on the whole river. People die running Crystal Rapid.

When Kyle's raft entered the Crystal, it was in the wrong position, and it was pitched over by a thirty-foot wall of water. Kyle found himself under the raft, trapped by his right hand. Cerebral palsy causes the body to do funny things sometimes, and once Kyle gets hold of something with his right hand, it's difficult to let go. He had gripped a rope attached to the raft and couldn't turn loose.

He rode Crystal Rapid underneath the raft, popping up into an air pocket to breathe. He then rode another rapid underneath the raft, and another. Riding through rapids like that underneath a raft is a recipe for disaster. It's a testament to Kyle's courage that he was able to keep his wits about him. One of the other members of the expedition dove under the raft, locked his legs around Kyle, and helped keep his head up in the air pocket under the raft. When he was finally pulled out safely, into another raft, he wanted one thing:

To get off the river.

Now.

He couldn't, though. There were eleven more days on the journey and no way to get off the river. I can't imagine the internal fortitude it would take to get back in a raft, knowing that your disability made a dangerous trip infinitely more dangerous, and face the remaining miles of river and rapids.

But that's who Kyle is. Although he's in a wheelchair much of the time, he walks on his knees, and he meets life head-on, absolutely refusing to allow his disability to define his existence.

He's been to base camp on Mt. Everest as part of the expedition that saw the first disabled climber reach the summit. He's climbed Mt. Kilimanjaro in Africa, and he's served as a whitewater guide in his home state of Idaho.

He has not only chosen to live his own life in that inspiring way, he's chosen to use his experiences to make the lives of other people better. He was the subject of an award-winning documentary called *An Uphill Climb*, which won him a Mid-America Emmy for writing, and is the author of a children's book called *Stare If You Dare*.

You know what Kyle's two greatest fears are? Water and heights. Really? When I first met Kyle, I said, "Hey, no offense, but if I was petrified of water and heights, I doubt I'd be whitewater rafting and mountain climb-ing."

His response?

"I can't run, I can't throw, I can't play sports. This is stuff I can do. Nature treats me the same as she treats everyone else. If I make a mistake on the river, I pay like everyone else. No more, no less. If I want to be a part of life, really *live* it, this is what I can do. I just have to face the fear. Once you do that a few times, you find out fear is fun."

His advice? Paddle like heck. And keep paddling. Kyle is a smart man.

So ride the rapids. Paddle like heck. And be exhilarated.

Okay, I misled a tiny bit with the title. This chapter is really about *acknowledging*. Man, I wish acknowledge was a cooler-sounding word. I wish the word boomslam, or BAM, or leathery, or even smangflangen had the same meaning. They're much cooler words.

Acknowledge, though, is a word that can take the stress out of nearly anything.

When you acknowledge that there will be challenges and bumps in the road, you can hardly complain when they happen, you know? If you acknowledge that sometimes things are going to go wrong, and sometimes they're going to be YOUR FAULT, it's easier to deal with things when they go haywire.

You know the difference between walking from where you're sitting to the door, and walking a thousand miles? A thousand miles is further.

There might be mountains, or rivers, or hot dog stands, or bears, or pretty little rabbits that look like unicorns. You'll deal with them. That's all part of the adventure. You just keep walking. Think of all you'll have seen when you get to the final destination!

If you pick a big, hairy, bodacious goal like walking

a thousand miles, **acknowledge** that it'll take a long time and will require more than you now have and more than you now know. You'll find it much easier to stick with it and figure things out.

As you look at your business, your life, your career, your college choice, acknowledge that it's going to be a challenge. It's actually not that big a stretch to think like that, because dang near anything that's worthwhile is going to be a challenge.

I remember one big, hairy goal of mine from the late 1980s and early 1990s. My students  and I decided to create a music video and send it to the leader of every country in the world. Keep in mind that we were from a very small high school in a very small community in the cornfields of southern Illinois. Not exactly a mecca for international communication, and certainly not a mecca for producing music videos.

It's not even like we had a lot of experience in the world of television. We weren't even a television production class! We were the high school band. In the middle of nowhere.

We knew we were taking on something big, and we acknowledged this project was going to require a lot of expertise and information we didn't possess. We simply didn't know how to do a lot of what we were going to have to do, but we jumped in, recruited kids, wrote lyrics and music, hired a film crew, and created a music video called *Together We Can*. Great—step one complete.

It wasn't easy, but it felt good to actually produce the music video and complete that part of the project. Then it occurred to us we had no idea how many countries there were in the world, let alone all their names. That would be easy to research today, but back then there was no Internet to look up things like that. Our school encyclopedias were no help, so we called the State Department and asked them.

They gave us the number of countries and a list of the names, and then we realized we had no idea who the leaders were. Someone told us the CIA published a book with the names of every leader in the world, so we called them and asked.

Sure enough, they had a book that was published every week. When I laughed about that, the guy said, "Oh, we have to publish it every week. The number and names of countries change, and so do the leaders." Hmmm, that was a new one for us!

When we received the book, we realized that some of the names were impossibly long. We also had no idea how to actually address them in a letter. Your Highness? Mr. President? Madame Secretary? Not to mention the actual physical address of each leader.

Hmmm again. I called the State Department again and finally found someone who had a list of every leader, how to address them, and their physical address. Perfect! Are you noticing a pattern here? When we didn't know something and couldn't figure out where to find it, we just picked up the phone and called. We called the White House, the State Department, the CIA, and television networks, and just asked to speak to someone who could help us. We found that people are generally pretty nice, and the worst thing that happens is someone says, "No." It's really not that painful, and once you've heard it a couple dozen times, the fear of hearing "no" pretty much loses its power over you.

So, we sent out the music video, and about fifty of the world leaders responded. It was so exciting! Here we were, in little old Teutopolis, Illinois, and every day there would 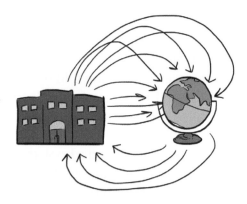 be envelopes from different world leaders. The president of the United States even sent us a letter.

We thought it would be cool to meet one of the leaders who responded to us, so when we found out the president of the Marshall Islands was coming to Washington, D.C., to open an embassy, I gave the embassy staff a call. They were wonderful people and were happy to help us, so about a dozen of us went to Washington and met with President Amata Kabua, the president of the Marshall Islands.

It was so cool for our students. The State Department had a training session for them so they'd know how to act with the leader of a country. President Kabua couldn't have been nicer and said he'd love to see us again. He also said he just wished people knew his country existed. As soon as we stepped out the door, we were all saying, "You know what would be cool? We should go to the Marshall Islands and do something there!"

The next summer, about a dozen of us went to the Marshall Islands and took a television crew with us. We filmed a student-led, student-hosted documentary about the Marshall Islands, focusing on its culture, history, and people. The Peace Corps put together a workbook to go with our documentary, and the package was sent out to about five thousand schools around the country.

Cool—a big hairy goal achieved! In fact, we went above and beyond achieving the original goal. *Way* beyond.

It didn't all go smoothly, though. Not by a long shot. We had money problems throughout the whole project, from the making of the music video to the trips to Washington, D.C., and the Marshall Islands. We had technical issues all through the shoot in the Marshall Islands. Our camera broke down … twice. First in Hawaii, thousands of miles from home, and then again in the Marshall Islands, thousands of miles from Hawaii! It wasn't easy getting a replacement camera, especially in the Marshall Islands.

In the end, though, we just kept going. We just kept walking, as it were. We created a vision of what a cool experience this would be, and we just KEPT WALKING. It was a thousand-mile journey and it wasn't easy. Was it worth it? Every person on that adventure would tell you his or her life was completely changed by the experience. *That's* how we chose to measure it—by the wonderful experience, not by the difficulties we encountered.

Remember the life lesson about using the magnifying lens in your life? You have to aim it correctly and acknowledge how challenging a big hairy goal might be. If you stay focused on what matters, on what is important, you can fight your way through all kinds of difficulties.

No matter who you are, no matter where you are, it's possible for you to dedicate the effort and creative energy to making big things happen. YOU control that. Embrace the experience, difficulties and all, and you can enjoy every step of the great adventure.

Things You Wish You Knew Yesterday

THE TOOLBOX OF LIFE

I've always been fascinated by the different ways in which we learn.

Some people take in information a bit at a time, process it, and then prepare for the next tidbit.

Others are able to grasp a big concept, which allows them to take in a whole bunch of stuff at one time. Some people gather things in a random way, connecting the dots as they go.

Still others seem to be able to connect dots between things that seem totally unrelated.

Our system of educating young people, a system more than three hundred years old, gives students the impression that learning is sequential and knowledge comes from the teacher. Really? We all learn differently, and we each have moments of clarity spurred by information or experiences that may be completely random.

Life steadfastly refuses to teach you things in order. Wouldn't it be nice if you could learn from life in a nice, orderly manner? Wouldn't it be nice if the information, skills, and experiences you need to succeed came in order?

But life gives you tools in a random kind of way, and sometimes you don't even know what the tool is for.

Heck, sometimes it seems like *life* doesn't know what the tool is for.

In school, if we tell a student, "Hey, this is a tool designed for this purpose, and this is what you do with it," kids will typically do that one thing and then set it aside.

There might be another need for that tool two minutes later and a student will think, "I already used that tool … there must be a different one."

We should be encouraging our students to recognize other situations in which that tool fits and look for brand new ways to use the same tools, ways that might never have occurred to the teacher. Who says the teacher is the "possessor of all knowledge," anyway, and who says we shouldn't expect students to figure out things on their own?

That's how something like the smartphone happens.

Do you think the smartphone was invented by people who believe that new ideas are the result of knowledge and information fed to you in an orderly, sequential fashion? If so, we'd have a phone that was easier to dial.

Somebody, or a group of somebodies, looked at the phone and saw things that weren't there. They saw technology that could be adapted, reimagined, repurposed, or invented to make the smartphone the incredible tool it is.

In your life, I challenge you to understand the tools you're given and look for situations in which you might use them. Embrace the tools you don't understand, put them in your toolbox, and keep your mind open for new ways to use them. Do that, and who knows? Maybe you'll be the person who comes up with the idea that changes *everything*.

Things You Wish You Knew Yesterday

FROM HERE TO THE DOOR

Many people worry that they don't have a "vision" for their lives. You want to know what it's like to have "vision"? Imagine yourself seated at a dinner in a large room, full of people. If I told you I'd give you a million bucks if you could walk from your chair to the door without falling over, would you be rich?

I hope so, but here's the point.

As you look from where you're seated to the door, your eyes and brain work together to quickly assess the risks. You instantly see all the possible obstacles in the way, and you calculate the best possible path.

You acknowledge the fact that you could trip, or some moral reprobate could trip you, or the ceiling could fall in, or you could have the tablecloth accidentally tucked into your pants. Some miscreant might have tied your shoes together without you knowing. Your brain could overload itself, thinking about all the things that could go wrong between you and the door. Frightening, isn't it? ISN'T IT?

For a million bucks, though, you're willing to accept all those risks. You're willing because you're pretty darn sure it's going to work out well in the end. I mean you can walk, right? That part of achieving your vision isn't that hard. You can do that while paying attention to all those potential problems.

That's how entrepreneurs think. It's not that they don't see risk, it's that they see *beyond* risk. They're pretty sure that whatever works out is going to be great, so that takes most of the anxiety out of it. They're convinced they can keep moving forward, recognizing and handling the challenges as they occur.

Creating a vision isn't really as hard as it sounds. The trick is to think over the top of all the perceived risks. How many times in your life have you thought of something cool, only to have it immediately quashed by a series of "Yeah, but what about?" questions that flash through your mind. Questions like:

"Where are you going to get the money?"

"You've never done that before."

"There are probably a million people who've thought of it already."

"Where are you going to build it?"

"What makes you think *you* can do this, anyway?"

"What if you fail? People will think you're an idiot."

About that time, the vision vanishes with a poof, and you feel kind of foolish about the whole idea.

If you can postpone the questions tied to all those risks, just for a little bit, you can imagine something pretty wonderful. *Then* look at the risks and measure them in relation to the big picture. You're not denying their validity, just holding them for the right moment.

Be an entrepreneurial thinker. Think big thoughts. Create a vision that excites you. You can think over the top of your actions, and you can remain focused on the goals as you deal with stuff that comes up. Try it.

It'll change your life.

Things You Wish You Knew Yesterday

THE BUCKEYE

When I was a teacher, I worked with kids of all ages, from kindergarten through high school, and in the fall it wasn't unusual to receive a special gift from a first grader just in from recess.

They'd run up, breathless, and say, "Mr. L, I've got something for you!" They would pull a buckeye out of their pocket, and with the most magnificent of smiles, they would hand it to me.

If they were a bit more articulate, here's what they would have said.

"This is the most beautiful thing I've ever seen. Look at all the shades of brown, and look how shiny it is. The more you rub it, the shinier it will get. You can carry it in your pocket, and it will bring you luck everywhere you go. Even if you never do any more than that, you can be happy knowing that I picked it out for you, and I gave it to you because I care about you, and I wanted to give you the very best thing I could find."

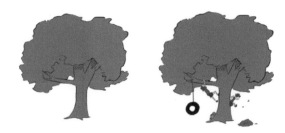

"If you plant it, maybe it will grow into a huge tree, and then you can climb it, and you can put a tire swing on it, and you can sit under it when it's hot. In the fall, you can pile up the leaves and jump in them. Any way you look at it, this is absolutely the best possible present I could give you."

The adult in us wants to temper that enthusiasm. We think to ourselves, "I'll probably lose it by the end of the day, and it doesn't really bring good luck, and chances are it won't sprout, and even if it did, by the time it grows big enough to climb or put a swing on it, you'll be too old to do stuff like that. And where you gonna get a tire, anyway? What do you know about actually putting up a swing, and what if the branch breaks? Who will be liable? There's an awful lot you don't know, kid, or you wouldn't be so excited over something like a buckeye!"

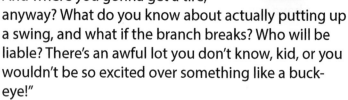

And even though we don't say exactly that, the child gets the message. And they look at that buckeye and think, "Boy, you're a lot of trouble, and who needs that? You're nothing but an ugly brown thing," and toss it aside. And the next time, they learn not to be so excited about imagining something wonderful, something full of possibility. They learn that you're supposed to focus on what is, not what *might* be.

Over the years, too many people grow up and buy into the notion that dreams are for someone else. If you can't fill in all the blanks ahead of time, if you can't answer every question before it's asked, if you can't be sure the dream you have today will come true in exactly the way you describe, exactly when you describe, exactly *how* you describe, it's not worth pursuing. In other words, you don't do what you don't already do. You don't try to learn anything you don't already know. You don't take the chance that something might not work out. You stay where you are, and you view everything you don't currently know as a threat.

You don't have to buy into that. Dream. Aspire. Achieve. You be the one who takes the buckeye, plants it, waters it, cares for it, and watches it grow into something amazing.

Things You Wish You Knew Yesterday

CHANGING THE WAY YOU THINK

It's possible that most of what makes our lives difficult is of our own making.

Things You Wish You Knew Yesterday

EVERYTHING HA$ VALUE

Over a thirty-four-year teaching career, I don't know how many times I heard it. "I don't see why I have to know this?!? I'll never need it!!! I don't see why I have to learn it."

Excuse me, but there's no need for everything to become apparent straightaway. In fact, it's not always someone else's responsibility to connect it for you. Some of the best, most innovative ideas come from moments where you use your intellect, life experience, and perspective on things to connect stuff that seems entirely "non-connectable." That often leads to something fantastic.

You forfeit the ability to connect that way if you close yourself off to information and knowledge in any particular moment.

Think about it this way. Let's say someone gives you a gold coin worth $1,000, and you're so stupid and shortsighted you say to yourself, "I'm not buying anything right this second, so I have absolutely no need for this. Why should I have to carry it around?!?"

So you throw it away.
Guess what, genius?
That coin is still worth
a thousand bucks. Its
value doesn't change
just because you don't
recognize it. Someone
else is free to pick it up
and use it.

STILL WORTH $1,000

Ideas, information, and learning are all like that.
They're offered to us through school, work, experiences, and people. It's up to us to recognize the value in
them. Even if we can't figure out the value right this
minute, surely we can see that they might have value
someday, right?

And it's true if you're on the giving end of the equa-
tion, too. If you offer kindness, ideas, information,
or whatever to someone else and they don't see the
value, that's okay. It doesn't mean what you offer is
without value—it just means that person isn't ready
or willing to learn from you right now.

So don't be the dimwit who throws aside something cool because you can't see past this minute. Take it in, invest it in your life, and be richer for it.

Things You Wish You Knew Yesterday

THE 3 MOST IMPORTANT THINGS

1) Do what you say you'll do

2) Do it when you say you'll do it

3) Communicate while you do it

If you do those three things, your life is going to be fabulously successful. Don't do them, and you'll join the legion of people who can't figure out why life is so complicated.

End of lesson.

Things You Wish You Knew Yesterday

NOBODY CARES ABOUT THE STORM ⛈

You know what drives me crazy? When people don't know the difference between getting something done and explaining why it's not done.

This approach to life has exploded in the last ten years or so. It's not just that people are willing to offer some cockamamie story about why things aren't done, it's that they seem unable to see the difference between that and actually getting things done.

They think to themselves, "As long as I can tell a good story, it's the same thing as getting it done. It's about a reasonable effort, not results."

Let's say you ask someone to make a call and get some information.

So they call, and nobody answers.

And they think,

In their mind, there's no difference between getting the information and not getting it. They put in a little effort, no one answered, and it's mis-

83

sion accomplished!

Excuse me, but describing the effort is not the same thing as accomplishing the task!
If you've been given the task to bring a ship safely into port, then bring the ship in safely!

It doesn't matter if there was a storm, or if your dog got sick, or even if you were distracted by an info-mercial called "Make your own spleen." It doesn't matter if you received a call from the president of the United States asking you to help solve some crisis in the world. Okay, maybe that matters. But except for something like that, you promised to bring the ship in. Period.

No matter how good the story, no matter how com-pelling the details, the person you promised is think-ing, "Yeah, but the ship isn't here, and that's what you told me would happen."

You're going to be amazed by how many times you hear this kind of thing in the next twenty-four hours. You may not have thought about it in these terms, but be prepared. People do this all the time.

Want to set yourself apart from most other people?

Do what you say you'll do. Do it in a way that people won't worry about some storm rolling in, because they know that if you say you'll bring the ship in safely, you'll bring the ship in safely. If you say it will be done, it's already *done*.

Think about that next time you start to spin a story about why something isn't done on time or done well. You'll stop yourself dead in your tracks and think, "Nobody cares about the storm."

Because they don't.

Things You Wish You Knew Yesterday

PERSONAL CAPITAL

As we do things in life, we acquire personal capital.

 Not like the building …

… but like the bank account.

When you do the right things, when you live and work the right way, you build capital with people. Like interest, it takes a long time to build, because it gains value slowly, over time.

Get it? Doing the right things once, or for a short period of time, doesn't go into the account, because people aren't sure it's real.

People can tell who you really are by the way you conduct your business, the way you treat people, and the way you live. Over time, those observations become their perception of who you are. They believe you to be a certain type of person, and they share that belief with others.

You can spend a lifetime building this capital, and the cool thing is that there's always room in the account for more. You can still be building it when you're ninety years old because the account is never full.

You spend it when you do something stupid. It doesn't seem fair. You spend so long building capital in your account, but it spends really quickly!

It spends a bit more slowly if you own your mistakes. In fact, if you handle it right, a mistake can actually *add* to your personal capital account. People will appreciate the way you handle mistakes and will give you credit for owning them. If you don't, though, it drains your personal capital account at a remarkable and alarming rate.

If you don't constantly reinforce your account with actions, that'll drain all the capital out of your account pretty quickly too. Think about it. Don't you know people who say all the right things? You give them an immediate deposit for that. How long does it take you to figure it out if they don't follow up with action? How long before you start to subtract it from their account?

The one thing you must never, ever do with personal capital is spend someone else's.

If you represent someone else—your family, your boss, your company—and you don't reflect the values and behavior people believe that person or company has, it reflects beyond you. The people you interact with may not even know you by name, so their disappointment is reflected back on the person or company they *do* know. That's incredibly unfair, isn't it? Don't you hate it when someone else does that to you?

So there it is. Live the right life, do the right things, do what you say you'll do, and you'll build a great personal capital account. Accumulate all you can, spend it as rarely as you can, and try NEVER to spend someone else's. That will give you an account that pays handsome dividends *and* helps you through the rough times in your life.

Things You Wish You Knew Yesterday

IGNORANCE VS STUPIDITY

We kind of use these two words in the same way, you know? When someone doesn't understand something we find to be obvious, for Pete's sake, we call them stupid. If we want to appear a bit more sophisticated, we use the word *ignorant*. Somehow that seems a bit more refined.

But ignorance and stupidity are actually two completely different things.

Ignorance is a lack of information. Someone who is ignorant isn't seeing the whole picture. Ignorance is okay. It's completely understandable and completely forgivable.

When someone says, "I don't see why," I like that they

actually admit their ignorance as they pose the question. You can usually fix ignorance by providing information. When someone gets clued in on the bigger

picture, they usually say, "Oh, okay ... I didn't know that."

Stupidity, on the other hand, is being ignorant on purpose. People who are stupid aren't really looking for information—that would only complicate things for them. They're happiest being ignorant.

Sometimes stupid people answer ignorant ones. I suppose we should be grateful when they find one another. Someone who is ignorant about something will say, "I don't see why ..." and the stupid one will say, "I'll tell you exactly why."

Wait—maybe it's not so great when they find each other.

Whatever the case, that's it. Be ignorant as often as you want, as long as you're open to information. Just don't be stupid.

THE THEORY OF MULTIPLYING

Ever feel yourself sinking under the weight of all the stuff you have to do? Stifling, isn't it? It feels like you have a bazillion things to do, and there's just no way you're ever going to catch up.

You're spinning in such a tight circle of busyness that you're unable to get anything done.

Try this: take a piece of paper (preferably a big one like a page from an art sketchpad) and list all the various headings in your life.

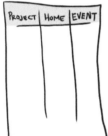

If you're a professional, your list might center on big topics.

If you're a student, it might revolve around individual subjects and activities.

Now list everything you have to do under each heading.

When I do this, I feel like I'm going to need lots of room to list all the things weighing me down. I just know it'll be hundreds and hundreds of pages!

But dang it, I can never, ever make it look as busy as I feel. I keep trying to think of things to add, but usually it just isn't that bad.

Generally speaking, we don't have that much to do. When we think about each thing a million times, though, they start to add up. Take eight things you have to do and think about them each a million times, and you'll feel pretty darn busy.

When you see it on paper, you'll realize how much time you spend thinking about how busy you are, and you'll realize you could spend that time actually doing the stuff you need to do.

One warning signal in my life is when some little thing comes up and I think, "That's all I freakin' need." When that kind of thought pops into my head, I know the problem is me.

Another is when I manage to include the words, "I'm so busy" in several conversations in a row. When I do that, I know the weight I'm dragging around is an inflated view of my sorry self.

Five minutes spent listing everything usually makes

me feel a little less full of myself, a little less like the weight of the world is on my shoulders.

As soon as you start to feel the press of busyness, take out that paper and cut the list down to size. I promise it will help you keep your life in perspective.

Things You Wish You Knew Yesterday

REPETITION IS GOOD
REPETITION IS GOOD
REPETITION IS GOOD

You ever sit in a desk at school, wishing you could raise your hand and say, "Uh, excuse me, but we already did this!"? I did. I couldn't understand, not for the life of me, why we went over things more than once. This is for a test, right? We took the test—we don't need this anymore!

As you work toward success in your life, you want repetition. Trust me. You want lots of repetition.

How do you think elite athletes get so good at what they do? Can you imagine a Major League Baseball player saying to the manager, "Hey, appreciate the chance for batting practice, but I did that yesterday. I get it. I'm supposed to hit the ball. Don't need to practice that every day."?

Baseball players know that repetition is the only way to really get good at what they do. Without it, they can't get to the next level of understanding. When certain skills become automatic through repetition, the player can think over the top of those skills. If he's not thinking about how to swing the bat, he can think of all the other variables, like what pitch the pitcher might throw, how many outs there are, how many runners are on base, and where the fielders are positioned.

Same in the field. I overheard a conversation in spring training a couple of years ago. A veteran infielder was talking with a rookie about fielding a particular kind of ground ball. The rookie was asking very specific questions about whether to back up or charge the ball. The veteran listened a minute and said, "You want to be really good at that? Take a hundred of those every day. You want to be better than everyone else? Take two hundred a day."

The veteran understood that if you field thousands of balls, you can predict what the ball is going to do before it does it. That kind of repetition frees you to see all of the possible outcomes as the ball comes toward you and allows you to think about what you're going to do with the ball after you field it. Powerful stuff.

In school and business, repetition allows you to anticipate problems and solutions, sometimes long before they become obvious to others. That's why some businesses seem to career from major crisis to major crisis, while others seem to avoid the train wrecks almost entirely.

So when you roll your eyes because some bit of knowledge or information is coming your way again, you're cheating yourself. Watch everything that comes your way. Notice the patterns. Notice the repetition.

That's how you know what's real.

Turn the repetition inward so you filter it through the lens of your own life and examine where you can apply what you're learning to what you do.
When you hear about the importance of customer service from fifty successful business leaders, you know it's *important*.

If you're a business leader and you hear the same complaint from fifty customers, you know you have a real problem.

When you embrace the value of repetition, you're able to think above/past/through a particular issue, evaluating whether it's something that can be fixed with a simple adjustment or whether you need to make a significant change to address it.

If you pay attention, you find patterns all around you. Sometimes you learn things you use in the same context, you see them in the patterns, and sometimes you see opportunities to use what you learn in a completely different way.

That's how medications are developed, stores are designed, websites are structured, and products are created: paying attention, watching for patterns, listening for commonalities, and doing things over and over.

See what I mean? It isn't complicated.

All you have to do is open your mind and pay attention.

All you have to do is open your mind and pay attention.

All you have to do is open your mind and pay attention.

THE KITCHEN OF LEARNING

Imagine yourself in a kitchen. You walk in with your head hanging, plop down on a chair, and a plate appears in front of you.

That's kind of the way school works. You show up, you sit down, and information appears in front of you. It comes from textbooks, lectures, and handouts, but you never really think about where it comes from. You just consume it.

Sometimes you're not even sure what you're being served. You don't really think about how it connects to anything, what it means, or even what you're supposed to do with it.

Get it? You're the consumer. You consume. You pretty much consume whatever you're served. Then you puke some of it back up on a test and you move on.

You know what's sad, though? If you never lift your head up and look around the kitchen of learning, you'll never know how all this happens. You could sit at that kitchen table and starve, never knowing that you have everything you need within arm's reach. There are cabinets filled with tools, knowledge, information, ideas, and lots of other cool stuff, and the cabinets are right there for you. Just as important, you'll never notice the people who prepare and serve all of it for you. You'll miss the opportunity to get to know them and learn how they do what they do.

Life is like that as well. You can sit at the table of life, head down, and just consume whatever is put in front of you. Things come at you in a way that seems random and disconnected, and you never move beyond just consuming whatever life gives you. It's shameful how many people live their lives like that.

If you just lift up your head, you'll find you're surrounded by everything and everyone you need to live a rich, satisfying, challenging life. You're surrounded by everything you need to take charge of your life and make exciting things happen. It's all there right now. Right this instant.

Lift up your head, explore the kitchen, and be amazed.

Things You Wish You Knew Yesterday

THINKING ABOUT HOW YOU SAY IT

Once you speak it, it's out there.

Words matter.

Things You Wish You Knew Yesterday

YOU THINK THEY DON'T KNOW?

I think it's fascinating that humans are able to hold starkly contrasting thoughts in their minds at the same time, pretending they fit together perfectly!

For instance, we think we have everyone else figured out. We're pretty sure we understand their motives, what they're up to, and what they're trying to put over on us. We're also pretty sure they can't figure out the same things about us.

And we have this sense that sometimes we get away with things because no one says anything to us about them.

Uh oh. Wrong. *Very* wrong.

We've all been on both ends of it, haven't we? Personally and professionally, we're very much aware of how others conduct their business. Based on what we see, we're constantly taking mental notes, evaluating, and making decisions about future involvement with that person. If we've noticed negative things about a person or a business—even if we never uttered a word about it—we file those thoughts away, and they guide our future interactions with them.

If we've noticed positive things about someone, those

thoughts are filed away as well. When an opportunity arises later on, we remember that person, and they move to the top of the list.

Let's say you promise to do something for a guy. Maybe you feel forced into it, maybe you don't want to do it, or maybe you have good intentions but never get around to it. Whatever. The point is, you don't get it done when you say it'll be done.

That's when the guilt sets in.

So when you see that guy, you do your best to avoid him. You know what I mean? Maybe suddenly you're on the phone with a very important imaginary friend. Maybe you skulk out of the room, hoping he doesn't notice you. Maybe you eat lunch somewhere else so you don't encounter him. It's embarrassing....

But eventually you run out of ways to avoid him, and one day you turn the corner, and there he is. You have a conversation, hoping he doesn't notice that your neck and face are turning red, hoping he doesn't notice you won't look him in the eye, hoping he doesn't notice how anxious you are to end the conversation and get away from him. Maybe he's nice enough not to bring it up.

You think, "Yessss! I got away with it."

You think he doesn't know?

Really?

He knows. People ALWAYS know.

They may choose not to confront you about it, but they know.

When someone pulls that kind of nonsense on you, *you* know, don't you?

Isn't it interesting that we think we know this about other people, but they somehow don't know it about us?

It's simple. If you say you'll do something, *do* it.

If you don't … *own* it.

It's your choice.

Just don't think they don't know.

Things You Wish You Knew Yesterday

QUIT IS THE UGLIEST WORD

There is a time and place, of course, where quitting is the only reasonable thing to do. Sometimes you have to stop the bleeding, take what you've learned, and walk away. You have to know yourself and the situation well enough to gauge whether it's best to call a halt to things.

I might even argue that pulling the plug and acknowledging failure on something isn't really quitting anyway. It's just wise. Quitting, in my view, implies a giving up, a refusal to devote yourself fully to something, a desire to find an easy way out of a difficult situation.

But holy cow, *quit* is an ugly word. Just look at it. It starts and ends with a harsh consonant. The middle of the word is an obnoxious "wuh" sound. Ick.

"Quit" is the most effective story killer ever invented.

Here, for example, is my story as a basketball player:

I was … terrible. I was the twenty-fourth man on a twenty-three-man, seventh grade squad. I was so bad I didn't even get a uniform. During games I sat in the bleachers, behind and above the players, and didn't even get to go into the locker room during halftime.

I wish the rest of my story went like this:

I hustled from the first minute to the last minute of every practice. I came early and stayed late. I shot five hundred free throws every night and went to sleep clutching a basketball. I was never a starter, but I got a uniform, and I scored eight points one game, the highlight of my career. I was determined to show my-self (and the coach) that I … could … PLAY.

That would be a cool story, wouldn't it? You want to know how my story really ends?

I screwed up the nerve to actually speak to the coach, and you know what I said?

"Umm … Coach, can I talk to you?"

"Sure, whaddya
need, kid?"

"Ummm … uh …
er … I quit."

(awkward silence)

"Okay, kid, thanks
for telling me."

That was pretty much the end of the story. The only thing I can say in my defense is that when I told the coach I was quitting, he looked at me as if to say, "You what? Oh, you were on the team?" I'm pretty sure he didn't look at me as a quitter. There's no doubt in my mind that he was relieved to be rid of me.

As you build the story of your life, just know that chapters like this sort of kill the story:

"I took a class last fall, and man it was hard!"

"Yeah? What'd you do?"

"I quit."

"Oh."

(awkward silence)

Or:

"I found something I'm really passionate about and

113

decided to start a business!"

"Really? How'd it turn out?"

"It was too hard, so I quit."

"Oh."

(awkward silence)

My advice for the big picture? Everything you do is part of the story you'll tell someday. Nobody tells a story that goes, "I had an idea, I made a fortune, everything worked, and then I retired." The ups and downs, failures and successes, all form the chapters of the story you'll tell.

Just think carefully before you create a chapter in your life that ends with the words, "I quit."

WHAT KIND OF CONVERSATION ARE WE HAVING? ;̈ ;̈

The good news is that *you* control what kind of conversation you have with someone.

Let's say you're a student, and you have a project due by email on Sunday night.

If you talk to your teacher on Friday and say, "I'm gonna be at my Aunt Erlene's this weekend, and she lives in a hut out in the woods and there's no electricity, no plumbing, a fire for cooking … so, I'm pretty sure there's no Internet."

That's a problem-solving conversation, and your teacher may well say, "No worries … just get it to me as soon as you can."

Let's say, though, that you wait until Monday to speak up. You say, "Umm … I didn't have Internet … and I just figured that … umm … I mean, I figured there was no point in telling you that … because … ummm … well …

115

there wasn't any Internet. I figured you'd just yell at me."

That, my friend, will spark a punishment conversation.

See the difference?

If you communicate when and how you should, you get to have problem-solving conversations.

If you don't, you get to have punishment conversations.

It works in other ways as well. Not long ago, my family and I vacationed at Walt Disney World in Florida. Our flight to Orlando, already late, was diverted because of weather, and we were very late arriving at the park for our first dinner reservation. Not a huge problem, to be sure, but it made for a very long day. There was a problem with our bill, because we had not checked into our hotel to activate the wristbands that guests use to charge their meals. The manager came to our table, listened to our story, and said, "It sounds like you've had enough troubles for today. I can't fix all that, but I can comp your meal and wish you a happy rest of the day."

The manager chose the conversation and turned a potentially frustrating situation into a delightful evening. That's one of the many reasons Disney is the fabulously successful company it is.

So *you* get to make the choice. It's okay to be mad if you choose a punishment conversation with your teacher, your boss, your customers, or your employees. It's okay to be exasperated if you choose to have a frustrating conversation with any of those people. Just don't be mad at them. *You* choose the conversation. You always choose the conversation.

Things You Wish You Knew Yesterday

YOU'RE NOT TALKING ⚫🍎 ABOUT THE SAME THING

There is a lot of pressure when it comes to making life decisions, like where to go to college, isn't there?

It's not like you're not busy already, with sports, home-work, work, and a million other things.

On top of all that, you have applications, scholarships, decisions about where to go, what to major in, what path your life should take.

It's overwhelming, isn't it?

Don't you wish your parents would get off your back?

Well, when your mom asks you, "Did you fill out that scholarship application last night?" you say, "Maybe if you'd quit buggin' me I'd do it!"

Nice.

Of course what you're *really* saying is, "You're right! I feel guilty that I haven't done it! I hope you understand I can't admit it, so I'm just gonna yell at you!!!" When you're embarrassed about not doing something you're supposed to do, how about owning it? It's funny when we try to say, "Why don't you treat me more like an adult?" but it comes out sounding like a spoiled five-year-old said it.

Nice, again.

You're talking about two completely different things!

What do you think your mom is thinking ten seconds before she asks the question?

She's thinking, "Man, I do not want to ask this … I already know the answer." She knows she's going to get barked at. She knows you're going to overreact. She also knows she has no choice but to ask. This is important stuff, and it has to get done.

So, she asks … you bite her head off … and you never realize that you and your mom are not talking about the same thing.

So, instead of owning it and saying, "Sorry about that, I'll get right on it," we yell. At someone who cares about us.

Nice, yet again.

You think she's on your case because you didn't fill the forms out last night. I mean, one lousy night!

She's talking about you living in her basement when you're forty!

See the difference?

You're having two different conversations. There's no easy answer here. Just know that sometimes when you have a disagreement with someone, it's because you're having two different conversations.

One of you may think it's about stuff that doesn't matter, like being a little late for something, and the other is talking about something big … like trust … or responsibility … or loyalty.

Remember when you burst into the house when you were younger and spewed some version of "My life is over!!!!" and your mom or dad kind of said, "It's no big deal"? You looked at them and said, "You don't get it. My … life … is … over." You felt like they were minimizing something that was very important to you, and that made you mad, didn't it? You probably either stomped off and slammed the door to your bedroom, or stayed there and tried to make them understand how deadly serious it was. To them it was about some minor problem of the moment. To you, it was about fitting in, finding your place in the world. It was about *mattering*.

Turn the tables. Remember a time when you were getting yelled at, and you were memorizing the pattern of the carpet, or your bedspread, or the top of your shoes? You were thinking, "Okay, I get it—for Pete's sake, let up!" You may have even said, "Okay, okay, okay, I won't do it again … can we just move on?" or something like that.

They didn't stop, though. They didn't stop until you cried or exploded in anger.

You know why? You weren't giving off the signals that indicated you understood the seriousness of whatever was going down.

Same thing when you were upset. You weren't getting the signals that told you your parents understood how serious it was.

Your parents were trying to help you understand that in the grand scheme of your life, the problem that day wasn't a big deal. They were probably right, too. A couple of days later you'd probably forgotten about it, and a month later you probably couldn't have even recalled what it was about.

When *you're* the one getting hammered on, you're trying to say, "I get it, it won't happen again, and can we please just get back to normal?"

You'd be amazed at how many hard feelings and conflicts come from this simple breakdown in communication. If you think about the person you're dealing with and really try to understand what they're saying, you might figure out the problem is you're not talking about the same thing.

Most of success in life is the ability to understand others, and the most important part of understanding others is to make sure you're both having the same conversation.

Things You Wish You Knew Yesterday

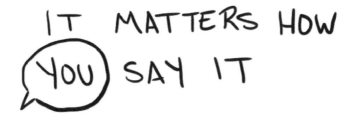

IT MATTERS HOW YOU SAY IT

Some people are more sensitive to tone and word choice than others, but everyone notices how you choose to say what you have to say. Have you ever walked away from a con-versation thinking, "Why the heck did they have to say it like *that*?"

When talking to other people, the words you choose and the way you deliver them have tremendous effect. Think about it. Say something simple like "Hey, nice shirt." With the right tone, that's a compliment. With a different tone, it's a complete insult.

My least favorite questions begin with the words, "Do I have to ...?" In my thirty-four years as a teacher, I never once answered a question that started like that. I always interrupted the student and said, "No, you don't *have* to. You don't *have* to do anything."

Try to pose a question that starts with "Do I have to?" and make it sound happy and sincere, not pouty and negative. Go ahead, try it out loud. No matter how cheerily you spin the tone, it's impossible.

Have you ever noticed when you ask a question that starts with "Do I have to …?" the answer is almost always preceded by a sigh?

"Do I have to help with dishes?"

(sigh)

"Yes."

You know why? When you start a question like that, the other person hears, "I don't want to." They're thinking, "All I'm asking is, in return for buying the food, cooking it, providing the table, giving you a place to live and sleep, that you help with the dishes. Yes, (sigh), that's what I'm asking."

It's simple, really. Start with "Would you like for me to …"

As in:

"Would you like for me to be there at 6:45?"

"Would you like for me to go to the store with you?"

"Would you like for me to go to your ballgame?"

Here's another one. Instead of saying, "I don't see why," how about "I wonder why?"

As in:

"I wonder why they funnel people into the stadium that way?"

Instead of:

"I don't see why we can't go in that way."

"I wonder" makes you open to ideas and information, open to innovations and solutions. "I don't see why" just advertises your ignorance.

Or:

"How would you like for this project to look?"
Instead of:

"I don't see how to do this."

You won't believe the difference in the way people respond to you. Thinking about this one simple piece of your communications can completely change the way people perceive you. They'll perceive you as supportive, encouraging, someone they can count on to understand them. They may not be able to put their finger on what it is about you that is so different from other people, but they'll like what they hear from you. And they'll be right.

Things You Wish You Knew Yesterday

I SAY WHAT I SAY!!!

There are countless fascinating things in this world, but nothing intrigues me more than the way our means and methods of communication are changing.

We should have the right to say what we want, right? But does it mean we're *obligated* to say what's on our mind?

When we can do it online, where it can be anonymous, people don't hold back at all, do they? I can't believe how personal and hateful it gets in that environment.

People seem to feel free to say absolutely anything that's on their minds, in any way that seems appropriate in the moment.

If we accept that premise, everyone else should be free to do the same thing, right?

Wait.

When we express our own opinion, we want to reserve the right to explain it, justify it, and assign our own tone to our own words. "When I called you an idiot, I didn't mean *idiot*. I meant 'eye-dee-aah-t,' like you're an idea person. I'm sorry you misunderstood, but I can't help it if you're an idiot."

When someone else expresses an opinion, that's different. It doesn't matter why they said it, when they said it, how they said it, or what they really meant. We examine it, pick it apart, assign meaning to it, and then let the world know how much we've been hurt by some specific piece of it.

How can we hold two such *completely* opposite thoughts about communication in our minds at the same time?

And the tone of our communication has to be right or there's trouble lurking on the receiving end.

We think we love texting because it has no tone. But when we text, if we don't use over the top things like "YOU'RE THE BEST!!!!!" or "See you there 🖤 😃 😃 " people wonder why you're mad at them.

I think we sometimes prefer anonymous posting on the Internet because it's nothing *but* tone.

We don't like to talk on the phone because, well, because we don't like to talk on the phone. We sleep with our phones, though, because if we don't answer a text in the middle of the night that person might think we don't like them.

So, we answer the text, then text another friend to complain about the first one, waking up the next friend who answers us because they don't want to hurt our feelings, but who then turns around and texts another friend to complain that we woke them up, who then … well, you get the picture.

Communication is at the heart of about ninety-five percent of the problems you'll deal with in your life. Improper communication, poor communication, lack of communication, they all contribute to the problem.

The answers to all problems relating to communication are relatively simple:

- Communicate clearly
- Communicate often
- Communicate appropriately

Life could be pretty simple if we lived up to those expectations. We probably won't, though, because we insist on being humans, and humans insist they know better.

I don't mean anything bad by that, really. I just mean humans are great 😃 and they're doing great things, and they're the best. 😃

I just wish we'd learn to be slightly better communicators.

Things You Wish You Knew Yesterday

UNDERSTANDING OTHER PEOPLE

**To discern the truth about someone else
is to see the truth about yourself.**

Things You Wish You Knew Yesterday

YOU OUGHTA SERVE HOTDOGS

You'd be amazed how many people think, because they like or don't like something, *everyone* in the world feels exactly the same way.

Picture it like this—a guy walks into a gourmet restaurant and says, "Hey, you oughta serve hot dogs. *I'd* eat one!"

Brilliant. The guy has no understanding of where he is, what they do there … nothing. He assumes that because he likes hot dogs, everyone likes hot dogs.

Right now. Right here.

In the years I've spent as a documentary filmmaker, dozens of people have come up to me and said, "You oughta do a documentary on such-and-such. *I'd* watch it."

Sure.

I'd be happy to spend the next couple of years working on a documentary so you can snooze in your

recliner for an hour on a Tuesday night.

If you want to be successful, start with the knowledge that your success will come from understanding *others*, not assuming they understand you.

I shared this life lesson with a very successful executive not long ago, and he said, "Uh oh, I have a lot of thinking to do." That poor man, who is in his sixties, has spent the last thirty years wondering why his employees are so thickheaded, why they can't understand what he's trying to get done. I suspect things around his company are different now, and much better.

Assuming that everyone thinks the same way you do is a recipe for frustration. You'll spend a lot of time wondering why life has to be so complicated, why people can't understand that *you* are the one who truly knows how everything should be done.

Listen to the conversations around you for the next day or two. Notice how many people seem puzzled by the world because everyone isn't just like them. You'll be tempted to interrupt and say, "You oughta serve hot dogs … I'd eat one!"

WHAT HAPPENS NEXT?

You know those moments you wish you could take back? Like the moment where you scream at your parents, "Okay, go ahead and ruin my life!!!!!!!!!" because they wouldn't let you do something you wanted to do?

It's not that you'd take back what you said, maybe, but you'd sure love a chance to say it in a different way, wouldn't you?

Once you've had a chance to think about it, yelling "Why won't you treat me like an adult?! I should get to do what I want to do when I want to *DO IT!!!*" and stomping out of the room probably isn't the most mature way to approach something. You probably miss the irony in the heat of the moment.

When you storm out after an argument with your parents, your teacher, your coach, or your boss, what do you think happens next? No doubt you think your mom or dad immediately goes back to *Wheel of Fortune*, (they're watching the sixth rerun of that show, for Pete's sake, and still can't figure out the answers to the puzzles), you think your teacher goes back to grading papers, and your coach or boss just goes back to figuring out lineups and work schedules.

Not true.

If you have two parents at home, they look at each other and say, "I don't know. Are we right? Should we argue about this?" If you have one parent at home, they're thinking, *I have no idea if I'm right—I wish I had somebody who would just tell me what to do.* Your teacher, coach, and boss replay the argument a million times in their minds, dissecting every word. "Did I say the right thing? Was I right to say it?"

You know what they're doing at 1:00 in the morning? Staring at the ceiling, asking the same questions, trying to figure out if they were right and just. Even if you've moved on (and you usually have), they're agonizing over it.

It's important to keep in mind that, in most of these situations, those people didn't do anything to cause all this. You did. You chose to make it a confrontation, not a conversation.

I know it's uncomfortable to hear this, but most of the time you control these situations. You have the ability to think and act reasonably, you have the ability to consider both sides of an issue, you have the opportunity to be classy and build some personal capital through the way you handle things.

Take the time to think about more than just your side of a situation. Take the time to consider someone else's point of view, and you may find yourself having completely different kinds of conversations than you're used to.

Things You Wish You Knew Yesterday

EVERYONE TELLS THEIR OWN STORY

Oh, the stories people tell. Some they tell about themselves, some they tell about others. You can take this to the bank; when something goes down, everyone involved will tell his or her own version of what happened, and there's a very good chance the storyteller will be the victim.

Let's say there's a conflict between a student and a teacher. It's something we've all witnessed in one form or another. After the incident, two completely different stories are told.

The student goes home and says, "All I was doing was sitting there. All I was trying to do is learn and better myself. You know, the country is depending on me to grow up and be the best possible citizen, and that's all I was trying to do. I don't know what happened—all of a sudden that teacher went crazy on me!"

The teacher goes home and says, "I was just trying to teach, right? Just trying to do what I'm supposed to do, right? Just trying to ensure our future one student at a time. Four years of college, years of experience, and all I'm trying to do is save that kid from himself. That kid sat right in front of me and stared at me like I had two heads. I'm not putting up with that!!!"

The point is simple; we all tell our version of the story. When there's a conflict, we do our best to paint ourselves as the victim. It's a natural human tendency; so, whether you're the "teller" or the "listener," just let it flow through that filter. It'll help you figure out where the truth in the matter lies.

There's a second, equally important side to this storytelling business, and that's the story people tell about you. Not gossip, mind you. (Ugh. Is there a more useless form of communication than gossip?)

I'm talking about the story someone tells after they meet you or work with you. They form an impression of you from that experience, and they file it away. It goes into the mental file cabinet marked "For future reference." If the story they file about you is positive, you may well find opportunities coming your way that you didn't even know existed.

I've seen it happen a thousand times. You're in a meeting or talking with someone, and an opportunity comes up, and you reach into that mental file cabinet and say, "You know who would be perfect for that?"

Nice.

I've also seen the time when, in the same circumstance, someone says, "How about so-and-so?" There is usually an awkward silence, and someone else says, "Hmm, you know, err, I just don't think they're right for this."

They're usually too polite to say what they're really thinking, but the effect is the same. You miss the opportunity, and you never even knew you were considered.

Ouch.

When you tell the story of some sort of conflict, make sure you really *are* the victim before you paint yourself that way, okay?

When you meet and work with people, make sure the story they tell about you when they leave is positive. Do those things, and people will hold you in high esteem.

I promise.

Things You Wish You Knew Yesterday

FOUR PEOPLE STANDING ON A STREET CORNER

There are basically four kinds of people in the world. If one of each was standing on a street corner, and the goal was to go out for dinner, here's how it would shake out.

Person #1 says, "I thought we were going out to eat, for cryin' out loud! How long we gonna stand here and talk about it? This is about food, not conversation!"

Person #2 says, "I need menus, locations, and information. Without all of that, I can't possibly make a decision, and nobody can make me!"

Person #3 says, "I don't care if we *never* eat. Just don't fight. It doesn't matter where we go."

Person #4 (who has climbed the street sign and is hanging upside down) says, "It's not about food, it's about *fun*. You all need to loosen up."

It's our natural tendency to think we do best when we're around people who are like us, who think like us.

Not true, and it's amazing how many people in this world don't get that!
You need to be surrounded by people who are different than you, who approach problems in a different way than you.

If all four people in the group were the same kind, here's what would go down.

Group #1 hasn't eaten. They fought over who got to make the decision, where they would eat, and what kind of food they would eat. They each figured everyone else would want the same thing they wanted. They're actually still standing on the corner arguing because none of them are willing to give in. They're all very hungry, of course, and somehow they know all this arguing is stupid, but none of them is willing to admit it.

Group #2 hasn't eaten. They're still on the street corner, with tons of menus all around them. They've accumulated lots of information, and they feel somehow there's an answer in there somewhere, but they're paralyzed by it because none of them really know how to move past gathering the info. They're so hungry they can hardly think, but they're so afraid of making a mistake, they can't commit.

Group #3 hasn't eaten. They're still standing on the corner, each of them saying, "Really, it doesn't matter. Whatever you want. Really. I don't care. Whatever makes you happy." They each have a pretty good idea where they'd like to eat, and they wish someone would just step forward and say it. They're all growing faint from hunger, but they're hanging in there because they don't want to offend anyone.

Group #4 is also not eating, but they're also no longer standing on the corner. They're in jail. They got distracted by something, forgot all about eating, and ended up doing something stupid because there was nobody to rein them in. They're not as unhappy as the other three groups because in jail they bring you food a couple times a day.

You need Person #1 to move the conversation toward some kind of solution. You need Person #2 to make sure it's an informed decision. You need Person #3 to make sure everyone is heard. You need Person #4 to make sure everyone has fun.

You need different kinds of people to make effective decisions and be successful. Recognizing the value in others is something successful people do every day. Seek out others who are different than you, and invite them into your world. Once you do, everything in your life is richer. You'll wonder how you ever got along without them.

Things You Wish You Knew Yesterday

LEARNING FROM OTHER PEOPLE

When you come across someone who has something figured out, pay attention.

Things You Wish You Knew Yesterday

PERSEVERANCE IS OVERRATED

Perseverance is a mostly misused word. It especially irritates me when people use it when talking about Thomas Edison. Okay, irritate is a strong word and, to be honest, I don't have tons of conversations *about* good ol' Tom.

Here's the thing, though. Ever hear the story about Edison that goes like this? "Edison failed a thousand times (or two thousand, or ten thousand) when he was trying to invent the light bulb. He persevered, though, and finally found something that worked!"

Well, excuse me, but he didn't persevere. He *expected* to fail a thousand times, or two thousand, or ten thousand. That was the plan all along. He didn't have to work through disappointment after disappointment, because he anticipated from the beginning that it would take hundreds and hundreds of tries before something worked.

151

Don't get me wrong. Thomas Edison was an incredible human being. He lived in a time when inventions were changing the world in profound ways. Telephones, automobiles, movies, and airplanes came out of his era: inventions that changed everything about the way people lived, thought, worked, and communicated.

He understood the huge implications of his work with the light bulb, and that certainly helped drive his work forward during the most difficult times.

You ever hear what Edison did after finding a way that worked? He tried a few hundred more. The guiding principle of his work was to exhaust every possible approach to the problem. The number of attempts was irrelevant.

When you don't acknowledge the obstacles and challenges, and embrace the knowledge you'll gain as you work through them, the work is just too hard.

Edison received more than a thousand patents in his life. That's incredible. He once claimed that his laboratory would turn out a minor invention once a week, and a game-changer every six months.

But not all of his ideas were great. He invented a vote-counting machine, for instance, that he tried to sell to Congress. It was so slow that Congressional leaders refused to buy it. They claimed it took so long to count that it gave politicians way too much time to argue, filibuster, and generally get in the way of getting things done.

Edison wanted to build concrete houses, where everything—sinks, cabinets, picture frames, tubs, beds, even pianos—would be formed from a single huge piece of concrete. He poured millions of dollars into the idea, and it limped along in one form or another for about thirty years. The venture, though, was mostly a disaster. It just didn't work.

So you see, Edison was a fearless inventor. He embraced the process and felt confident that whatever turned up in the end would be great. If it wasn't, he was confident another great idea would come toddling along out of the wreckage.

It's fear that keeps most of the people I meet from approaching life like that. They're petrified that what they do, or think about doing, might not be right. That's too bad because that kind of fear the creative process that produces ideas and solutions.

If you know there will be failures and vow to learn from them, you'll focus on the goal, not the individual failures. It frees you from the daily worry of "What if this isn't right?"

That's a powerful approach to life, both personally and professionally. You may or may not ever invent something as important as the light bulb, but who cares? The life you create for yourself will be productive and challenging; and trust me, what you do will matter.

CONTROL ONLY WHAT YOU CONTROL

Todd Frazier plays for the Cincinnati Reds. I've known Todd since his first day as a professional baseball player.

I was filming a documentary about Cobb Field, a Minor League Baseball stadium in Billings, Montana, and Todd and I showed up at the stadium about the same time. He changed into uniform, my crew and I unpacked our camera gear, and it turned out the first thing we filmed was his first workout as a pro, and I've followed his career closely ever since.

I started doing behind-the-scenes documentaries with the Cincinnati Reds during the 2010 season, and Todd's first call up to the Reds came during the 2011 season. I joked with him once that I made it to the big leagues before he did, and someone immediately said, "True, but Todd gets paid better."

Touché. Well played.

Todd is a first-rate baseball player, but that's not what I admire most about him. He's a wonderful human being. I've marveled over the years at his enthusiasm, his energy, and his positive attitude.

It's easy to say, "Focus on the things you can control and let go of the rest." It's pretty tough to actually live that way, but it's precisely what Todd does.

On his journey through the minors, he couldn't control who stood between him and the majors. He couldn't control trades, couldn't control when the big league club felt he was ready for the major leagues. In baseball, he knows he has no control over the following things:

- When he plays
- What position he plays
- What the pitcher does with the base ball
- What happens to the baseball after he hits it
- What other people do or say

What he can control is his approach to his work. A positive attitude? That he can control. Great work ethic? In his control.

After a great spring training in 2012, Todd made the big league club and traveled to Cincinnati to open the season with the Reds. Coolest thing ever, right? Culmination of his dream, right?

Not exactly.

Late in the afternoon of the day before Opening Day,

the Reds saw an opportunity to pick up Alfredo Simon, a pitcher who had been released that afternoon by the Baltimore Orioles, and that meant Todd was the odd man out. He would have to go back to the minors.

Bitter pill? You bet. Turmoil on the inside? Of course. What Todd chose to do, though, was go back to the minors, play as hard as he could, and be ready when he got his chance.

A very short time later, an injury opened a spot for Todd and he got the call to return to the Reds. Over the course of the season, he filled in at third when regular third baseman Scott Rolen was injured, and then became the regular first baseman when superstar Joey Votto injured his knee. Todd helped carry the team during that stretch and had a lot to do with the Reds winning the NL Central Division that fall.

When the playoffs came, everyone was healthy and Todd returned to the bench. Easy? No. How did he handle it? He worked just as hard, cheered his teammates on, and looked for every possible way to help make the team better. He understood and acknowledged the things that were beyond his control and put them aside to concentrate on being a great teammate.

After that season, he was selected the National League Rookie of the Year by the other players in the league. He became the regular third baseman for the Reds, a team leader, was named a member of the National League All-Star team, and was the National

League champion in the Home Run Derby.

Guess who was named to the All-Star team with him? Alfredo Simon, the same pitcher who caused Todd to go back to the minor leagues when he signed with the Reds. Guess who was the first player to congratulate Alfredo Simon? Guess who cheered him the loudest? Todd.

Todd Frazier is the rare human being who seems able to sort things out and completely release the parts that are out of his control. It's amazing to watch.

Ever met anyone like that? If you have, just watch and learn, my friend. Watch and learn.

IN ONE HEARTBEAT

BA-BUM

Sometimes you have a pivotal moment in your life, and you *know* it's a pivotal moment. A job interview, a marriage proposal, a huge presentation—you know those moments can change everything.

Sometimes your life pivots, and you can only pinpoint it in retrospect. When I was a freshman in college, I glanced up at a particular moment and spotted the girl I would marry. It took six months to find out her name was Beth and start to worm my way into her life, but both our futures pivoted in that moment.

When Beth finally agreed to the whole marriage thing, I knew I would need a job to support us while she finished college. Someone in her dorm said her hometown was looking for a band director, and in that moment our lives pivoted again.

I thought I would teach for a couple of years and then do what I really wanted to do: go to Los Angeles to be a studio musician and songwriter. I never expected to get totally hooked on working with kids. We didn't buy a house and even lived in a furnished apartment so we wouldn't have to buy furniture. We didn't do any of the things that people our age did, because I wanted to believe that I was still free to go to Los Angeles and pursue my dreams. I never did, though. I could never actually leave my students. Once I accepted that teaching was going to be a long-term part of my career, my life pivoted again. I focused on combining my creative and professional drive to create cool experiences for my students. That satisfied my creative ambitions, but more importantly, it allowed me to give students the opportunity to do and experience things they never thought possible. The realization that I could never leave my students shaped every professional thing I've done since.

One of the most remarkable things about Beth is that she's been okay with all of it. I've learned a lot from her over the years. She's taught me, by example, how to live a life that is centered on others as opposed to myself. She's shown me how to be genuinely committed to others, and how to love, forgive, celebrate, and appreciate each moment. She's a kindergarten teacher, which I suppose is logical for someone like her, and she has completely supported all the crazy stuff I've done over the years. I can't recall a single occasion when she complained about any of it.

Sometimes she even participates in the craziness. Our life pivoted again one summer when she spent about eight weeks on the road with me. I was the music director for an international children's show, and Beth was the unofficial "mom" for the cast of kids from all over the world. We toured the East Coast of the United

States, and she cared for those kids, worked in a show business world she never thought she'd be a part of, and proved to be invaluable to the show.

If you check back to the life lesson called *Boomslam!*, you'll find the story of my students producing a documentary about the Marshall Islands. There are a couple of sentences in there about having camera troubles while in the Marshalls. The rest of that story? It was incredibly difficult to get the replacement camera to the Marshall Islands. We went to the airport every day, hoping to see the camera. Every day we heard the same response, "Maybe tomorrow."

I stayed close to the telephone and the airport while Beth and my parents, who were also along for the trip, planned things to keep our students active and engaged. They traveled to a neighboring island, arranged dinner with President Kabua, and found ways to get our students involved with Marshallese students.

Our time was growing shorter and shorter, and there were serious doubts about completing the project. The replacement camera finally arrived in the Marshalls, on the flight we were scheduled to take out of the country. The camera crew and a couple of us stayed behind to finish the filming, and Beth agreed to take the rest of our group back to Hawaii.

When that flight was ready to depart, Beth and the group prepared to board via a staircase attached to the plane. Beth, who is a very petite woman, refused to get on board until she actually saw the camera. I'll never forget the sight of this big airplane on the runway, ocean on both sides, and this tiny woman who wouldn't get on board until the crew proved they had the camera. Amazing.

I could share a hundred stories like that, in which Beth was totally focused on the success of others; ready to take on anything to help them accomplish their big goal.

In 2003, we shared a completely different kind of experience, and everything pivoted again in a single heartbeat.

Doctors had seen something suspicious on Beth's mammogram. No big deal, just something to check out. With each appointment and new test, our concern grew, but we remained hopeful it would just be a scare.

Then came the phone call from the doctor.

When you hear the word "cancer," the world stops. It literally feels as though the world stops turning. It's forever between one heartbeat and the next. In one heartbeat you have fears, but hope everything will be fine. The very next heartbeat, everything has changed. You have immediate questions, like, "Which doctor do we see next?" and long-term questions like, "She'll survive this, right?"

In that one heartbeat, though, something magnificent happens. Life is crystal clear. You can see exactly what matters and what doesn't. Instantly. Let me tell you something: very little really matters. Most of life is just stuff. It ain't cancer. Literally.

Beth and I are so grateful for that moment of clarity.

Not for what brought us there, mind you. I won't lie—the experience was terrifying. It was also empowering. Beth experienced the depth and breadth of people's love and concern for her, and it made her even more committed to living an other-centered life. As a matter of fact, she decided that she would not only survive the diagnosis, she would do well during the process. At every stage, doctors and nurses talked about how remarkably well she handled everything. It didn't surprise me, because she decided beforehand that she would do well. Interesting how that works, isn't it?

Beth has now been cancer-free for more than ten years, and I've watched this remarkable woman use what she's learned about life to help other women through their own diagnoses. She reaches out to them, cries with them, encourages them. There's no doubt in my mind that other women have had a much better outcome in their own cases because of what Beth shares with them.

I wouldn't wish Beth's experience on anyone, but I hope you have moments of clarity like that, where things crystallize in a heartbeat. Write down what you've learned in that moment and keep it to read again when you really need it.

In the bright light of that single heartbeat, you'll know

things you never knew before.

PEOPLE MAGNETS

When you're a junior or senior in high school, and again when you're a senior in college, you live in a very odd, in-between world, don't you? You're not really an adult, but you're not a kid. You don't really want to be a kid anymore, but you're not nearly ready for everything that comes with being an adult.

Guess what?

Some of it you figure out as you get older, and some of it you *never* quite figure out.

Pieces of adult life—like taxes, insurance, and mortgages—are figure-out-able. They're all just details of one kind or another, and every adult figures them out one way or another. You ask questions, you get help, and you deal with them as you need to. It's part of the day-to-day fabric of your life.

Dealing with people, though, isn't just details. Well, actually, it is about details, but not like you think. Interacting with other people is mostly about understanding, acknowledging, and dealing with the details of who they are, how they think, how they act, and how they communicate. Fail to do that, and you may find yourself mired in a world of frustration, resentment, and conflict.

165

It's one of the most difficult things we do, because people insist on being human beings, and human beings are, frankly, challenging.

It's like you're in a play your whole life. The actors change, but the characters in the play remain constant. You can never really get totally away from any particular kind of person, because they're *everywhere*, so you better learn to deal with all kinds.

We'll call the first guy "I. M. Nofun." You know this guy? He gets wound up over meaningless details and makes your life miserable unless every single little thing goes his way. You might be tempted to say, "You know, for ten cents, I'll shave your eyebrows," just to give him something else to think about, but it probably won't change his demeanor.

Let's call the next person "Idontgetit."
She refuses to see any details at all. In
fact, she seems out of touch with anything normal. She's waxing philosoph-
ical nonsense about some grandiose
notion, completely ignoring the fact
that her hair is on fire. When you point
it out, she says something like, "Oh,
no worries. Everything is lovely. By the
way, what's that awful smell?"

How about "Mustbenice"? He doesn't really do a lot
in his life. He makes himself feel better about that by
cutting down what you do. He makes comments like,
"Must be nice. If I had that kind of time, you should

see what I'd do!" or "Must
be nice. If I had that kind
of opportunity, you should
see what I'd do!" He acts as
though everything you've
done has somehow been
taken from him and given to
you.

You ever met "Dag" (short for Doom and Gloom)? Dag
sucks all the energy out of you the
instant she appears on your radar.
It feels like you're a balloon, and
the knot that holds you together is
coming loose. You can almost feel
the "pfft" of all your enthusiasm
draining away. Sometimes you
even make that little sound a balloon makes when the air is coming

out. You know, that *phweeeeaaaaaooooo* sound.

Thank goodness there are people, though, who have the opposite effect on you. They radiate energy. They see the big picture of your life and appreciate hearing about the details. They *get* you.

When you're around a person like that, you complain a little less, stand a little taller, and act a little nicer. You feed off of them, like a hummingbird feeds from a bird feeder.

They're people magnets.

I think at the heart of it lies the fact that people magnets don't require anything from others. They value others; they enjoy others, but don't exact any kind of payment in return for being around others.

That's why they radiate energy. Their ability to be truly interested in others attracts people to them. It attracts opportunities to them. It makes them seem really, really smart.

Think of it this way …

If you look through the little end of a pair of binocu-lars you see a very small piece of the world. It's easy to think only about how it impacts and affects you.

If you just turn them around, you see a huge piece of the world, and it's easier to think of things you can do, can influence, and can be a part of. It's a completely different view of the world.

Being a people magnet makes it infinitely easier and more productive when you find yourself in a new situation, especially if it involves accepting a promo-tion, assuming new responsibilities, or taking over a leadership position.

One of my favorite people magnets is Karen Forgus, who is the senior vice president for business operations with the Cincinnati Reds.

In her position, she does business in the hundreds of millions of dollars. Baseball, when you think about it, is at its core an event business, and the Reds host eighty to a hundred ball games, plus over two hundred other events, each year at the ballpark in Cincinnati. Karen oversees ticketing, sponsorships, marketing, communications, graphics, promotion, social media, community relations, broadcasting, broadcasting rights, and a dizzying array of other things.

It's a lot of pressure, for sure. It's too much to expect one person to know every detail about every one of those areas, and Karen doesn't. Because she's a people magnet, she's able to draw the best possible performance out of the hundreds of people who do the day-to-day management of all that.

Being a people magnet is precisely what led Karen to this opportunity. She had worked in radio for years, and in 2006 had to make the decision whether to go full-time with her work or look for something new.

Someone said to her, "Hey, the Reds are looking for someone to do public relations stuff. You should go talk to them."

That's the way it works being a people magnet; people look out for you, people want good things for you.

She talked with the team owner and accepted the position. Between the time she accepted and her first day, though, the owner changed the job description and her title. She would now be a vice president!

Karen said, "Umm, we need to talk. You should know that I don't absolutely love baseball. I'm more of a carpool mom, not a vice president."

The owner said, "Karen, we need to reach people who don't really love baseball, and if you can understand them and reach them, you're exactly who we need. If I don't give you a big title, nobody will let you into the meetings. You need a title to get a seat at the table."

Karen and the Reds want to create a baseball experience that makes people want to come to the ballpark every year, whether they're baseball fans or not. If the Reds accomplish that, she knows the business side of the organization will be successful. To do that, it's critical that Karen understand not just the process but also the people who work for the Reds.

She spent the first year attending meetings, letting people know she was there to listen and learn, not to announce a new "Karen" policy. Interacting with hundreds of people at all levels of the organization, she was able to make them all shareholders in the work of the team.

By understanding what was important to them, she was able to share the vision of the organization and help them understand how they fit into the big picture. By listening to them, she was able to develop these core values for the Reds business operations.

Reds front office employees should be:

- Resourceful
- Collaborative
- Innovative
- Accountable

Karen also understands who she is and what value she brings to her work. That's a hallmark of people magnets. One of her most valuable skills is to understand multiple sides of an issue, opportunity, or situation, and present options for decision-making. She's a listener and a discerner, and she's focused solely on doing the right thing for the Reds, their employees, and their fans. Like other people magnets, she sees far beyond how things affect her personally and consistently looks at the bigger picture.

It's working. Attendance is up, and the ballpark is well known as one of the cleanest, most fan-friendly, and most fun in Major League Baseball. The staff is customer focused, and they have a clear vision of what the Reds are all about. It's amazing what a people magnet can do for a business.

Karen has people magnets she gravitates toward as well. She says, "I ponder what they say and do. I make lists of the things that mean the most to me about those people, and I think about why they are like they are."

Want to be a people magnet? Live a life that is focused outward, a life that is focused on other people, on ideas, on things that are positive. You're able to see the best in others, and you're much more able to forgive faults in others. Do that consistently, and people will find themselves eager to be around you.

Think about the people who are the magnets in your life. Study them, ask them how they do it, and make that part of your own life. Like a lot of other great things in life, and everything in this book, it's not complicated … it's just hard.

Things You Wish You Knew Yesterday

EPILOGUE

I hope you'll come back to this book. And come back often.

You're different every day. You pay attention. You learn. You grow. You understand things you didn't the day before. Things you *couldn't* the day before.

Come back and read again and again. Absorb each of these chapters from the vantage point of where you are a month from now, a year from now.

Whatever you've picked up from reading this book, know this: you can't go back to the person you were before you read it. The revelations you've had, the thinking and pondering you've done—they've changed who you were. Even if you wanted to, you couldn't go back to not knowing what you now know.

So go and do. And do well.

Things You Wish You Knew Yesterday

ACKNOWLEGEMENTS

Acknowledging is something that takes the stress out of big, bold goals. Acknowledging also allows one to be truthful about one's work by recognizing those who play a vital role in any successful venture.

It's not fair that one name is listed on this book as an author. The true authors are the wonderful people who have taught me these essential truths about life through their words and actions. Thank you to everyone who has shared, in one way or another, wisdom about life and success.

Dean Samuel is the first person I ever heard share the lesson called *Nobody Cares about the Storm.* You've changed a lot of lives with that one, Dean, and thank you for sharing your wisdom.

Jessica Parmenter's brilliant illustrations help the stories come alive, and it's a thrill to collaborate with a former student in ways that are meaningful far beyond the pages of this book.

Every young person I ever had the privilege of working with, young people from all over the United States and all over the world, contributed to this book in their own unique ways, and I thank each of you. I don't dare mention any of you by name, but many of you will surely see your reflections in the words I've written. The same is true for the great teachers I've worked with over the years.

Thanks to Meggie Zahneis, Gregg Lohman, Kyle Packer, Niall and Kristie Campbell, Todd Frazier, and Karen Forgus, who graciously allowed me to share their stories in the book. Thank you for living lives we can learn from.

Without the watchful eyes and well-used editing pens of Meggie Zahneis, Sarah Horner, Janet Grunloh, Lisa Houston, and Beth Lindvahl, the book would have been much less readable. Thank you for your knowledge and expertise.

Bronwyn Hemus, special thanks to you for the eagle-eyed proofreading that corrected so many things I didn't know were wrong.

Midland States Bank, through its investment in the future called the Midland Institute for Entrepreneurship, has changed my life. Thank you to Leon Holschbach and the rest of the board and senior leadership for the opportunity they've given me to pass that on by changing the lives of others.

The board of the Midland Institute for Entrepreurship: Jack Schultz, Karen Wolters, John Perles, Bob Schultz, Sharon Schaubert, and Audra Schultz. You've put your confidence in my work and seasoned it with your expertise and guidance. That has provided a mission and passion that will carry me for the rest of my life. Same goes for Susan Hanfland, Liz Roepke, and Tyler

Yocum, my Institute family.

My real family-Ron and Ann (my dad and mom), and Mark and Kim (my brother and sister)-have lived much of what I've shared in this book. It's easy to recognize the most important things in life when you grow up surrounded by them.

My wife, Beth, not only allowed me to include her in this book, she has allowed me to be a part of her life. It's the single best thing that's ever happened to me.

Things You Wish You Knew Yesterday

About the Illustrator:
Jessica Parmenter

One of Craig's many former students, Jessica has continued on into her professional life seeking creative opportunities. Currently working full-time as a graphic designer, she fills her spare time with side-projects and going on adventurous outings with her dog, Ozark.

Things You Wish You Knew Yesterday

Want to know more?

visit **www.MidlandInstitute.com**

www.WishYouKnewYesterday.com